Leonard Bernstein

Notes from a Friend

SCHUYLER CHAPIN

Walker and Company
New York

First published in the United States of America in 1992 by Walker Publishing Company, Inc.

Published simultaneously in Canada by Thomas Allen & Son Canada, Limited, Markham, Ontario

Library of Congress Cataloging-in-Publication Data
Chapin, Schuyler.
Leonard Bernstein: notes from a friend / Schuyler Chapin.
p.   cm.
Includes index.
ISBN 0-8027-1216-9 (c)
1. Bernstein, Leonard, 1918–   . 2. Musicians—United States—
Biography.   I. Title.
ML410.B566C5   1992
780'.92—dc20
[B]   92-15738
                                                          CIP
                                                           MN

Frontispiece painting of Leonard Bernstein by René Bouché appears courtesy of The National Portrait Gallery, Smithsonian Insitution.

Book design by Shelli Rosen

Printed in the United States of America
2 4 6 8 10 9 7 5 3

CONTENTS

✠ CONTENTS ✠

FOREWORD

Bernstein and Chapin. I knew one; I know the other. Curiously enough, I only rarely saw them together. They make as surprising a pair as Dr. Johnson and Boswell, especially as separate personalities now joined in a delightful memoir.

Leonard Bernstein lived his life at the top of his lungs, one of nature's sprinters if ever there was one, whose lavish expenditure of energy and talent was an endless act of generosity toward his audience, friends, or those unknown to him. Even his quiet moments took on the character of a subdued shout. In the custom's shed of opinion, he declared everything he possessed every time, down to the contraband, the whole sparkling with shafts of a rare intelligence. One remembers the moment that the engineers decided they were compelled to rerecord the opening bars of a Bruckner symphony because Lenny had inserted a drumroll not marked in the score. It was, of course, no drumroll at all but the Maestro stomping on the podium to launch the orchestra on its initial effort.

Schuyler Chapin is a man very different by nature, endowed with an enviable lucidity and the extraordinary ability to adapt himself to circumstances almost invariably challenging. Before most of his friends knew him, he was flying planes to China during the Second World War, as part of the American effort to aid Chiang Kai-shek. I can neither imagine him in such a role nor imagine him doing it less than brilliantly. He was at different moments head of the Masterworks Division of Columbia Records, program director of New York's Lincoln Center, general manager of the Metropolitan Opera, and dean of the School of the Arts at Columbia University, to say nothing of his multitude of jobs acting in various capacities on this or that committee or jury.

I have seen him against many backgrounds, including those of the lavish Renaissance gardens belonging to an Italian branch of his family. It was there that I recognized the fact that had he been immensely wealthy, and the Duke of Mantua to boot, he would have been an unparalleled patron of the arts, with impeccable taste, Schuyler the Magnificent, probably poisoned by a jealous condottiere after having succeeded in negotiating Michelangelo's exclusive services for ten more years.

I must say I prefer him as he is, a man with a gift for friendship unique in a world of shifting values. He is a father, but also a pal, to an array of talented sons, and he is the husband of the superb woman who was once Miss Betty Steinway. This is a family, in every sense of the word, that needs no pious phrases from those seeking election to eulogize it.

Finally, what is so eminently satisfying about this book is that it does full justice to Leonard Bernstein's genius, but in doing so, and despite the author's rampant modesty, it also inadvertently does justice to *his* genius, reticent perhaps, and endowed with humanity, but breathing life between the lines.

—Sir Peter Ustinov

PREFACE

The genesis of this book was a February 1991 memorial service for Leonard Bernstein at my church, All Souls Unitarian in New York City. Although Jewish by birth and basic faith, Bernstein was nonetheless fascinated by other religions and found special pleasure in Unitarianism. He often visited All Souls and regularly read the sermons of Walter Donald Kring and the present minister, F. Forrester Church. At Forrest Church's invitation he once delivered a Sunday sermon, choosing as his topic the power of love. Those present that day are not likely to forget the passion of his convictions.

Shortly after Bernstein's death, Forrest and music director Walter Klauss asked me to prepare a Sunday memorial service devoted to his life; I was honored to do so. Samuel S. Walker, Jr., and his wife, Beth Walker, were in the congregation that morning, and a day or two later I was surprised to receive a letter from Mr. Walker asking me to write a book.

I immediately replied that I thought it awkward to undertake such a project since I'm one of the three executors of Leonard Bernstein's estate, but after consulting with my fellow executors and with his three children, who were encouraging, I met with Mr. Walker to find out just what type of a book he had in mind. When he told me he wanted a souvenir "for all those people who sat in all those seats for all those wonderful years of concerts, theater, and television," the invitation was irresistible.

The result is what you now hold in your hands. It's not a biography, not a series of musicological explorations, not a confessional or a book of gossip. It's about a man who perhaps more than any other single individual in our lifetime brought excitement, dignity, vitality, and world recognition to American artists. Over many of these years I was privileged to help him in his work and to know him both as an artist and a family man.

Next to my own wife and children, I think Leonard Bernstein was the most liberating influence on my life. He taught me never to be afraid of passion and never to stop exploring the world. He was the older brother I never had, the teacher I'd always missed. He was also my friend.

With affection and love I dedicate this book to Leonard and Felicia Bernstein's three children—Jamie Bernstein Thomas, Alexander Bernstein, and Nina Bernstein, and to the two young Bernstein grandchildren, Francisca and Evan Thomas, who one day will know all about the extraordinary heritage from which they spring.

Leonard Bernstein

O N E

Good-bye and Hello

Leonard Bernstein was a great believer in what one might call serendipity of the calendar. November 14, for example, was an important day throughout his adult life: On that date in 1937 he met Aaron Copland, who became his first mentor. On that same date in 1943 he made his unexpected and, as it turned out, historic debut with the New York Philharmonic. And it was on 14 November 1954 that he made his first television appearance on "Omnibus" with a never-to-be-forgotten analysis of the first movement of Beethoven's Fifth Symphony. It's not an exaggeration to suggest that these three events turned out to be important not only for him but also for all American music.

I never realized until recently just how much our friendship, too, involved coincidence. Leonard Bernstein and I first met on 14 October 1959 at the National Airport in Washington, D.C., upon his return from his triumphant European tour as the newly minted music director of the New York Philharmonic. I was there as the new director of Masterworks for Columbia Records, then his exclusive recording label. On that day we began a professional association that developed over the years into a deep personal friendship, lasting until his death in the early evening of 14 October 1990, thirty-one years to the day since we'd first shaken hands.

Airports were where our particular adventures often began and ended—Berlin, London, Los Angeles, Munich, New York, Osaka, Paris, Rome, San Francisco, Tel Aviv, Tokyo, Vienna, Washington, and even Martha's Vineyard. On the afternoon of 14 October 1990, as I was preparing to leave Kennedy Airport for a flight to Zurich and Hamburg, I was profoundly worried about his poor physical condition. This was to be a business trip for my employers, Steinway & Sons, ending a week later in Tokyo, where, among non-Steinway responsibilities, I was to stand in for him to receive his Japan Art Association 1990 Praemium Imperiale award for music.

I was uneasy about this journey because just five days earlier his lawyer, Paul Epstein, his manager, Harry Kraut, and I (Harry and I being sole trustees of his business affairs) had divided up a list of his closest friends,

2

calling to tell each of them about his acute emphysema and decision to retire from conducting.

To add to my anxiety, I hadn't seen Lenny for several months—actually only once since we'd returned from a 1989 trip to Israel. For some reason he kept putting me off; we'd talk on the phone—we had to do a fair amount of that because of business matters—but anytime I tried to make a personal date, he'd demur.

The single exception to this odd behavior came in January 1990, when President Bush offered him the National Medal of Arts. He first accepted this honor, then rejected it when John Frohnmayer, former chairman of the National Endowment for the Arts, rescinded a grant to Artist Space in New York for an exhibition relating to the AIDS epidemic.

Lenny's rejection of the president's medal caused a big flap in Washington, exacerbated when Frohnmayer changed his mind and reinstated the Artist Space grant. By that time the maestro had already written a letter to the president explaining his views, but it was too late; Bush was in no mood to reinvite him. I was anxious he not make a big public brouhaha about this incident; the arts themselves were under fierce attack from some members of Congress plus a clutch of right-wing religious groups and I didn't think Bernstein gasoline needed to be poured onto already raging fires in the politicized cultural arena.

I insisted on seeing him early one evening at the height of this crisis. When I arrived at his apartment, he was sitting in his study. I made my case for diplomacy rather than his customary climbing of the barricades; he listened quietly to what I had to say, and when I finished he showed me his letter to the president, as well as separate ones he'd written to each of his fellow honorees, explaining his actions. The letters were masterpieces of articulate reasoning couched in dignified and elegant language. "That's all I intend doing about this business," he said, smiling and looking me right in the eye. "Please don't worry!"

I, of course, had no idea this was to be the last time I would see him, but I did know that something did not seem right when we took off together for the 1989 Israel trip. As the trip progressed, so did my sense of foreboding.

A word of explanation here about Bernstein and Israel: in a lifetime filled with enthusiasms and obsessions, one of the constants was the State of Israel and the Israel Philharmonic. To him the orchestra was an article of faith, the musicians playing in it fighters for freedom in the same sense as the nation's citizen-soldiers. Beginning in 1947, when they were known as the Palestine Symphony, and instantly in 1948 after Israel was established as a nation, and almost every year thereafter, he gave his services to the orchestra, either in Israel itself or by taking them on world tours. He was a major force in shaping the group into a splendid ensemble.

By 1989 he had a number of Israel Philharmonic recordings in various catalogs; he now wanted to record some Hindemith with them, including the *Mathis der Maler* Symphony and the *Symphonic Metamorphosis*. Harry Kraut was unable to take the trip; he and Lenny telephoned to see if I might be free to go. Lenny reminded me that in all the years we had known each other I'd never been to Israel. I was delighted to accept the invitation.

The trip began with a Concorde flight to London that was eight hours late. When we finally arrived in London, in a state of travel exhaustion, we faced the usual Bernstein chaos: within the next twenty-four hours a large reception and dinner given by Deutsche Grammophon, a press conference, meetings with various impresarios about future plans, and a steady stream of assorted nabobs, friends, and supplicants flowing in and out of his Savoy Hotel suite. But this time something was different: I could see that his vaunted energy and enthusiasm were flagging, and he was often racked by a dreadful cough. He looked worn out; deep circles under his eyes were set off by almost translucent skin drawn tight across his temples. Often he'd turn away from what he was doing and, uncharacteristically, just stare out the window.

A couple of days later we boarded an El Al flight from London to Tel Aviv. We were the only people in first class, and once we were under way he seemed to ease out of the doldrums, attacking his favorite English crossword puzzles, enjoying his Scotch, talking volubly to me and the cabin stewards. Yet there was something amiss, something almost desperate about all this. I knew he'd been seeing his doctors—usually that didn't mean too much, just endless talk about every possible hypochondriacal ache and pain—but when I asked about his latest checkups he fobbed off my question.

Before I could ask again, he changed the subject and plunged into a lecture about Israel whereupon his frailties once again vanished. He gave me a capsule history of the country, beginning with the Balfour Declaration and ending with Yitzhak Shamir. He reached into one of several briefcases, taking out a recent copy of the *Jerusalem Post*. "This is one of the great newspapers of the world," he said. "The editor is a good friend. I want you to meet him, and I also want you to meet Teddy Kollek." And he went on about other friends, his eyes clear, his voice strong, his enthusiasm contagious. But he finished by saying he didn't know if he'd have the energy to make all the arrangements, and then, quite suddenly, he was talking about our friendship, about his children, about composing and performing, about the state of the world. It slowly entered my mind that he was, in a very real sense, summing up his life. I pushed such thoughts away but couldn't shake the vague feeling of uneasiness.

When we arrived in Tel Aviv, we were met by a delegation from the orchestra, including the manager, a pleasant-visaged fellow named Avi Shoshani, and Yossi Falk, a short, burly reserve sergeant in the Israeli army who was Lenny's driver whenever he was in the country. The sergeant quickly caught my attention: he looked at Lenny long and hard and evidently didn't like what he saw. I watched him glance over at Shoshani and then at me. His face was a map of concern, but before he could say anything the usual flood of luggage arrived and we were on our way to the Tel Aviv Hilton.

After settling the maestro into his suite and turning him over to his traveling manager, Craig Urquhart, who had arrived the previous day from America, Shoshani, Falk, and I had a cup of coffee in the Hilton lounge.

"So what's wrong with our Lenny?" Falk asked, as soon as we sat down.

"Nothing," I replied. "He's just tired from the long trip."

"That's not new," replied Falk, "he's always running around. No, this time there's something else."

Shoshani interrupted with some details about the upcoming concerts, and we were joined by the recording team from Deutsche Grammophon, who had musical and administrative questions of their own. Falk, however, our conversation unfinished, never took his eyes off me.

Rehearsals began the next day. The orchestra was unfamiliar with the Hindemith scores; knowing this, arrangements had been made for first readings to be done by the young conductor and Bernstein protégé, Michael Barrett. I went with Michael to the morning sessions and was surprised at how truly awful the players were: sloppy entrances, ensembles rushed and often out of tune, and a number of muttered, unpleasant exchanges. I was impressed by how well Michael handled this difficult situation, including one moment when he felt compelled to remind the entire ensemble that they had come unprepared and that Maestro Bernstein was not going to be happy unless they shaped up immediately.

In the afternoon Bernstein took over. I was sitting behind the brass and timpani and, after the first few bars of the *Symphonic Metamorphosis*, could see the displeasure spread across his face. However, instead of the usual conductorial grimaces, his eyes swept over them like those of a rabbi surveying an obstreperous congregation. Patiently he explained who Hindemith was and why his music, mostly ignored these days, was important. Then he proceeded to break down the work section by section, and, in some cases, note by note.

At the first rehearsal break I sat with him while he had a cigarette and numerous swigs of bottled water. "They've never played this music," he commented, "and it's difficult." I murmured something about the obligation of professional musicians to overcome such difficulties and to be responsible and prepared. He held up his hand. "This is an orchestra with no replacements nearby. Think what they do here, surrounded by enemies, where the nearest fellow musicians are hundreds of miles away. It's a miracle they play at all.''

As the afternoon progressed his teaching, pleading, and coaching began to bear fruit: the music began to coalesce from notes and forms to sounds with structure and shape. I could see the musicians themselves react to the changes—they sat straight in their chairs. The exchanges heard now centered only on improving musical matters. Bernstein had restored their pride as artists.

As it happened the rabbinical outlook did not end with the day's rehearsals. Motoring back to the hotel he reminded me that Passover began that evening at sundown—I'd been invited to join the seder at the home of his friends Lewis and Aviva Harris and their considerable family. Knowing this to be my first Passover celebration, he began explaining the ceremony to me, his fatigue from the afternoon's work seeming to evaporate as he did so.

By the time we arrived at the Harrises' apartment, I was dizzy with the details of tradition and Lenny was fairly bursting with joy and exuberance. Not surprisingly he knew all the words in the service that is read around the dinner table to commemorate the exodus of the Children of Israel from Egypt. He also, of course, knew all the tunes, not only those used by American Jews but European chants and Oriental songs in a wide variety of languages. The Harris family seemed to appreciate his enthusiasm, although they were probably a bit startled by his assuming command. To me, his fervor that night was the first sign I'd seen on this trip of the old Bernstein energy in full force.

Orchestra rehearsals continued over the next days and gradually the musicians began to sound like a cohesive group; from there it was a short step to performance.

The concerts themselves were all being recorded, and at the conclusion of each work on the program, Hans Weber, the record producer, would come to the maestro's dressing room, score in hand, to make his comments. Weber, tall and white-haired, with wire eyeglasses and ramrod posture, always wore a tie and jacket for these discussions and brooked no nonsense from anyone else who happened to be in the room. I noticed Lenny always paid close attention to him. "Mein lieber, lieber Hansl!" he would say, discussing various changes needed in repeat performances. It was obvious Weber had become his alter ears.

At the end of each concert there was the usual postconcert tumult—old friends crowding into the room, young musicians wanting a few moments of the maestro's time, steely mothers with determined children, the occasional sob story, the autograph collectors, all pushing forward to touch, hug, embrace, and kiss him. He sat in a comfortable chair behind a sturdy table, naked to the waist with a thin robe over his shoulders and a towel wrapped around his neck. Sweat poured off his body as he smiled, talked, greeted, smoked, and drank his Scotch. I watched from the side of the room as this hustle and good-natured camaraderie went on for an hour or more. I'd seen it often before; this time I thought his spontaneity was sometimes on automatic pilot. He just didn't have his old verve. He didn't look well.

Two concerts later, just before beginning the last piece on the program, he turned to me. "I think I'll pull a Karajan tonight," he said, referring to that particular maestro's fixed habit of never greeting his public and always leaving the concert hall immediately after his last bow. "Let's have supper at the hotel. I'm really tired." I looked at him; in all the years of our friendship I'd never heard him make such a suggestion before. I didn't like it, even if those endless dressing-room soirees were often exhausting and tiresome. "You really want to do that?" I asked. He smiled. "Yes, and I mean right after my last bow, just like Herbert."

And that's what he did. Craig Urquhart had his towel and robe ready, together with a cigarette and a Scotch, and we went from the stage to the car, driving straight to the Hilton.

It was at that particular supper, which we had sent up to the Bernstein suite, that I became convinced something was indeed seriously wrong. Craig and Michael had joined us. Lenny sat at the room-service table, shoulders hunched, hardly speaking at all. When the food arrived, he pushed it around his plate. Occasionally he would smile at some remark, but most of the time he just sat there. Finally, excusing himself, he walked slowly toward his bedroom door. He turned at the doorway and looked back at the three of us; with a shock I suddenly realized he was becoming a frail old man.

A few hours later, unable to sleep, I went back to his suite. I had a key; it was not necessary to knock. The living room had the leftover smell of uneaten supper. On the piano were scores and manuscripts of partially completed projects, an ashtray filled with cigarette butts, scattered pencils, and music paper piled in a vague semblance of order on either side of the piano bench. Then I heard the coughing—heart-wrenching gasps and the sounds of gulping for air. I went to the bedroom to find him bent over, reaching to find some pills. We just looked at each other. I went to the bathroom, returning with a glass of water. He had the pills in his hand. He swallowed the medication, drank the water, took my hand, squeezed his thanks, and collapsed back onto the bed.

"What about a doctor," I asked, reaching for the telephone.

"No. No doctor," he said softly. "No doctor. We'll be home soon."

The next day he didn't get out of bed until late afternoon. He suggested I join him for his breakfast, out on the balcony of his suite overlooking the Mediterranean. He was little rested but seemed to want to talk about his personal affairs, a subject he rarely mentioned.

Something in what he said during that late, brown-horizoned afternoon moved me very much, and in a rush of feeling I looked over at him. "You know you're one smart son of a bitch," I murmured, "and I love you a lot, but you've organized your life in such a way that everything you own is in the hands of just three friends, three disparate friends like Harry, Paul, and me. You trust us with your life!"

He smiled, looking genuinely amused and also a little puzzled. I suddenly felt compelled to tell him a story about his daughter Jamie and her new apartment.

The story was simple: Jamie and her husband, David Thomas, were at that moment expecting a second child; their apartment was simply too small for a family of four. Several weeks before our trip, Jamie had asked her father if arrangements could be made to purchase larger quarters. The papers for such a transaction were drawn up, but reading them over I noticed that there were no provisions for her brother or sister. I pointed this out to my colleagues, telling them that I, as the father of four sons, never made any family financial agreements for one without being immediately prepared to do the same for the others. Harry Kraut and Paul Epstein, neither of whom have children, were a bit bewildered; they responded with resounding denials of having had any such exclusions in mind, and pointed out that the other two children had no need for such funds at the moment.

13

I said that the money had to be available now regardless. "You set something up for one," I insisted, "you've got to set up the same thing for the others. It's called *per stirpes*. It's what keeps families from falling apart!" I spoke heatedly and sent my two colleagues back to the drawing board. Two drafts later we had the right document and I signed off.

When I finished my story I wondered if it might sound mundane to him. Apparently not, for Lenny leaned across the table and, reaching out, patted both my cheeks. "Why do you think you're there?" he said.

I was moved, as always, by his confidence. Everyone in his life had a special role, and Lenny used all our strengths and skills to advantage.

Two days later we packed and drove to Jerusalem for the last concert. As we went along the scarred road from Tel Aviv he told me hair-raising stories of the War of Independence, pointing out various memorials along the highway as we proceeded up to the holy city. On arrival we booked into the King David Hotel and there, waiting for us all by himself, was the mayor of Jerusalem, Teddy Kollek.

Our arrival happened to coincide with the opening ceremonies marking the fiftieth anniversary of the beginning of the Holocaust and, as evening approached, we drove with Kollek and the late Yossi Stern, an Israeli painter and a friend of Lenny's, to Yad Vashem to mark this awesome occasion.

14

At the memorial, I was overwhelmed by the ceremonies honoring a large group of surviving non-Jews who had helped Jews escape from the Nazis. The non-Jews were from every European country imaginable, including Germany and the Soviet Union; as each in succession stood to be acknowledged by the enormous crowd, we were deeply moved. Lenny was in tears, as was I, as, indeed, were Kollek and the rest of our party, but the tears dried up when Yitzhak Shamir rose to speak.

I understand only a word or two of Hebrew, but I could see by the expression on Lenny's and Kollek's faces that Shamir was blasting someone or something. Yossi Stern began hissing a translation into my ear, and as he did I was horrified to learn that Shamir was saying that what the Nazis did fifty years ago would pale by comparison to what Arabs would do to Israelis, given the chance. I watched Kollek—the man who had rebuilt the city of Jerusalem by amassing private funds and bringing together Jew and Arab in a common cause—slide down in his seat. He covered his eyes, shaking his head, and muttered something to Lenny, who reached over and hugged him.

Later that night, after the ceremonies were over, we drove to the best restaurant in Jerusalem, La Rotissiere at Notre Dame. Paul Epstein, who was in Israel on other business, had arranged this dinner in advance and planned to join us. La Rotissiere happens to be in the Arab section of the city. Earlier, Avi Shoshani, knowing of these plans, begged me to persuade Lenny to change his mind; he felt that he shouldn't be seen in Arab Jerusalem that night of all nights, and that he might even be in danger of attack from extremists. Lenny would have none of this, and asked Teddy Kollek to join us. Kollek said he'd look in for dessert and coffee, and a couple of hours later, accompanied by Paul, he did. When he walked into the restaurant, the warm pleasure on the faces of the waiters was vivid proof of his personal success in bringing people together.

Kollek spent the evening trying to persuade Lenny to compose an opera about King David. As I sat listening, I came to see how he had managed to talk people into giving hundreds of millions of dollars for Jerusalem's restoration—he was tender, witty, commited, and seductive. Tired and tense as Lenny was, I could see his eyes sparkle at the prospect.

Toward the end of dinner, Kollek almost had his agreement when he was interrupted by the restaurant owner approaching our table; a whispered conversation between the two of them lasted a minute or so, and then with a shrug Kollek rose to leave. "Duty calls," he said, waving good night and walking slowly out of the restaurant. I was surprised that there were no police or bodyguards visible.

The next night was the final concert of the trip, the performance taking place in a ghastly modern auditorium having all the charm of an unused gymnasium. The orchestra and the maestro struggled against poor acoustics and an indifferent public; Hindemith was definitely too strong a taste for Jerusalem concertgoers. Nonetheless, the evening ended with great applause and a standing ovation for Bernstein.

Of course none of us knew then that it would be his last appearance in the country he loved so much, but looking back I wonder if he didn't have some kind of premonition. As the orchestra members streamed into his dressing room for their traditional good-byes, his personal farewells seemed highly charged, more emotional than I'd ever seen. I remember thinking that it seemed of a part with the unusually wistful and reflective behavior I'd seen throughout the trip. And, of course, there was that persistent, hideous cough.

An hour after the concert we were en route to Ben-Gurion International Airport for a 2:00 A.M. flight to New York. The departure terminal was absolute bedlam, in the middle of which we spotted Kollek; he was taking the same flight. The sight of him cheered Lenny, and we all passed together through airport security. Once on the plane Kollek settled into his seat and was asleep in an instant. "God, I envy him," Lenny said. "I can never sleep on airplanes."

But he did that night, after an inedible dinner, several Scotches, and a clutch of pills. I looked over at him from time to time, head leaning against the window, his mouth open, listening to his raspy breathing and occasional snores. Once again I was struck by his frailty.

As the endless hours passed I dozed occasionally, at one point slipping into real sleep. I know because I awoke suddenly with a start, uncertain where I was until I turned and saw Lenny. He was working on a puzzle, glasses halfway down his nose. His face was in repose and I wondered whether I was reading more into his condition than I had cause to do. But this reflection ended abruptly when he was seized with a coughing fit, his face turning crimson, his body doubled with pain. I put a hand on his arm, but he looked straight ahead, gasping for breath.

In a moment a steward appeared; I sent him off for a glass of water as Lenny pointed to one of his handbags. I opened the lid—the case was filled with medicines of every description. He pointed to one box of pills and held up two fingers just as the water arrived. I took out two, which he grabbed, stuffing them into his mouth between gasps, somehow managing to swallow a mouthful of water.

Presently the seizure came under control. He put his head back on the seat, utterly exhausted, and closed his eyes. I watched him for a few moments, my heart in my mouth. There was no question: my friend Leonard Bernstein was seriously ill. This proud, beautiful man was shrinking before my eyes, the once clear features twisted, the face craggy with lines of pain.

When we arrived in New York, Harry and a limo were waiting. We collected our baggage, said good-bye to Kollek, who was off to Columbia University, and moved out into the terminal. Lenny insisted on giving me a lift, and when we said our good-byes I hugged him hard and asked him when he was going to see his doctor. "Tomorrow morning," he said quietly. "And one more thing— thank you, dear Schuy, for all your help. We'll see each other soon." And he kissed me on both cheeks.

As I said at the beginning, except for the "diplomatic" visit in January 1990, I never saw him again. But as I also said, he was very much on my mind when I left for Europe on the late afternoon of 14 October 1990.

That afternoon my plane took off on time, an increasing rarity these days, and after a comfortable dinner I'd just settled down to read when the purser approached. "Mr. Chapin, we have a message for you from the flight deck. You are to call your wife as soon as we land in Zurich." I sat for a moment not saying anything; the purser stood alongside until I acknowledged his message.

I began thinking hard. It was probably not a family matter. It was unlike my wife, Betty, to send a message to me on an airplane; she would wait until I'd reached my hotel. That left only one real possibility.

A Swiss Air attendant met me at the gate in Zurich and took me immediately to the post office, where I called home. Betty gave me the news: Lenny had died at 6:15

19

P.M. She had tried to reach me at Kennedy but was too late.

We talked a few minutes as she filled me in on the details; we both decided, heavy heart or not, that it would be wise for me to continue my trip. The funeral was to be two days later, at his apartment, and I knew she'd be there, together with three of our sons.

When we'd finished talking I put down the phone. There was just a lone operator on duty at that hour, who must have sensed something was wrong. When I left my booth she looked at me sympathetically. For some reason I told her that Leonard Bernstein had just died; she clasped her hands to her mouth. We stared at each other for a moment as tears started down my cheeks.

I had an hour between planes and wandered around the Zurich airport in a daze. Finally, as I sat in the waiting area for my flight to Hamburg, my mind began turning back to another airport at another time, all those many, extraordinary years ago.

T W O

A Special Magic

The National Airport in Washington, D.C., always makes me nervous. This has nothing to do with flying; it has all to do with the impedimenta of modern-day travel—I won't be able to find a cab, the hotel will have messed up my reservations, the person I've come to see will have been rushed to a hospital minutes before our rendezvous—these kinds of fantasies dominated my thoughts on 14 October 1959, the day I was to meet Leonard Bernstein for the first time.

I was in Washington to be on hand when the New York Philharmonic returned from a highly successful European tour that included the orchestra's first appearances in the then Soviet Union. I had just begun my job as director of Masterworks at Columbia Records and was more than a little nervous about making contact with the famous maestro, who had, only the year before, been appointed the Philharmonic's first, and to this day only, American-born music director.

There was also one major glitch in my new position: somehow or other Columbia Records had failed to notice that Bernstein's personal contract had expired in mid-September and that the New York Philharmonic's had also finished up at the same time. There were, of course, red faces and wan smiles, but facts were facts and they'd been handed on to me some three weeks earlier, almost my first day on the job. It was my responsibility to see that Bernstein and his orchestra did not leave the label.

The Philharmonic's tour had been a resounding tri-umph—in Greece, Lebanon, Turkey, Austria, Poland, Holland, Germany, Luxembourg, France, Switzerland, Yugoslavia, Italy, Norway, Sweden, Finland, Great Brit-ain, and in the USSR, where Bernstein especially endeared himself to the public, if not the Soviet authori-ties, by talking to his audiences before performing, and speaking out generally about artistic freedoms. *Time* magazine said the tour was "likely to go down as the most successful of all time." One Western European newspa-per commented that with the "New York Philharmonic's playing of U.S. and Soviet music on the same program the international stage was set for the forthcoming meeting of Eisenhower and Khrushchev." A little too expansive, perhaps, in light of Francis Gary Powers and his U-2 spy plane, not to mention the cold-war problems that continually plagued the world until the 1990s, but we must consider that back in 1959 the 1990s were barely even dim specks on distant horizons.

It was understandable, then, that there was restless anticipation on the part of all of us gathered at the Butler Aviation terminal to welcome the orchestra home. Those were the days before international jets, when graceful Boeing Clippers flew at a leisurely pace, looking for all the world like airborne yachts, and, on landing, taxied slowly, even majestically, to their terminals. As the Philharmonic charter approached it was easy to see a lot of happy faces jammed against the plane's windows.

It wasn't long before I caught my first glimpse of the slight, elegant maestro, running down the ramp and into the arms of everyone in sight. I remember what he was wearing—gray slacks and a blue blazer, with a smart ascot around his neck—and that he seemed to be sparkling with energy. Directly behind him came a breathtakingly lovely woman, slim, blond, her face wreathed in smiles, looking a bit bewildered but entirely cheerful. She, too, was surrounded by people eager to embrace her. Later we were introduced: she was his wife, Felicia.

I inched forward into the happy mayhem and was swept up by the press, eventually finding myself in a tight circle of working cameramen. Having been told who I was, the Bernsteins looked over in my direction. They both waved, the maestro indicating he wanted to talk and pointing to his limousine. Felicia pointed as well and slowly began making her way toward the car. We both arrived at the same moment, just as mounds of luggage began to appear. I stepped awkwardly over several sprawled suitcases, and we shook hands. Her smile melted my nervousness.

"Lenny wants you to ride with us to the hotel," she said. "Hop in and make yourself comfortable." I did. The maestro sat in front and turned to me. "Is my contract all settled?" he asked as fellow passengers squeezed and shuffled for sitting space. I said talks were still going on. "Then I have no contract," he said, frowning. I replied it was only a matter of ironing out a few details. "But why isn't it done?" he asked, and began telling me about George Marek, then head of RCA Victor, our biggest rival, who had been to see him with an offer of any orchestra he wished and whatever repertoire he chose to record. "Did you know that?" I replied that I'd heard rumors. "I want to be free to record whatever I wish," he said. "I don't want anyone telling me such and such cannot be done. Right now I want to record the Shostakovich Fifth before we open our New York season. We have some dates in the south next week and finish the tour in Boston. I want to record the work in Symphony Hall." He was polite and absolutely definite.

I knew he was performing the Shostakovich that night in Washington. It had been one of the sensations of the tour, the final Moscow performance given in the presence of the composer and a group of the composer's friends, including Boris Pasternak. I also knew that the likelihood of recording the piece in Symphony Hall—the home of the Boston Symphony, then under contract to RCA Victor—was dim. Both the orchestra and RCA were jealously protective of the superb auditorium, never allowing any other record company to use it.

But I was undaunted. One of my fellow passengers in the car was John McClure, Masterworks music director. When we arrived at the hotel (and there actually was a reservation for me!), we put our heads together. McClure recalled lending RCA the organist E. Power Biggs, an exclusive Columbia artist, to record the Saint-Saëns *Organ* Symphony with Charles Munch and the Boston a year or so before. That meant that the BSO and RCA owed us a favor. I called Tod Perry, the Boston Symphony's managing director, and Alan Kayes, my counterpart at RCA, and told them what we needed. After a bit of waffling, they both finally gave permission, and we fixed the recording date. Bernstein's first challenge had been met.

That night we all went to the concert. The hall was sold out and every inch of standing room filled. It was a gala crowd—the vice president, the secretary of state, diplomats, congressmen, senators, Washington society, the works—the atmosphere was festive and anticipatory.

When Bernstein came onstage the crowd roared; he bowed and smiled. At just the right moment he turned and raised his hands to begin, and the audience instantly quieted down.

At intermission there were lots of conversations about the crispness and precision with which the orchestra was playing; people wondered how this could be after such a long and difficult tour. But the true test would come in the second half, devoted entirely to the Shostakovich. The newspapers had been full of reports about its reception in Russia and the composer's enthusiasm for the sound and energy given the piece by the Americans.

With the playing of the symphony, all expectations were fulfilled; the excitement never flagged and, with the last movement, its heroics and fanfares in full cry, Bernstein made the work more compelling than ever. At the final chords the audience leapt to its feet, the cheers almost bringing down the plastered ceiling of Constitution Hall. I was on my feet carrying on with the rest and vastly relieved to know we were going to record it while it was still fresh in the orchestra's repertoire.

After the concert a group of us gathered backstage and eventually moved on to a party at a house in Georgetown. Once again I rode in the car with the Bernsteins, and as we were walking up the steps of the house the maestro turned to me. "Is everything arranged for Boston?"

I looked at him for a long moment and answered, "Yes."

"You mean it's really all set?" He sounded as if he didn't believe me.

"Yes," I answered, and gave him a brief summary of what had happened.

"Oh boy, are we going to be friends!" he replied. With that he was swept into the house and into his hostess's arms.

That night was the first of a long line of experiences with the Bernsteins at parties. Most of the guests flocked around him, but Felicia was by no means left unattended. She was surrounded by admirers all evening; her smile and charms were hard to resist.

As I watched both of them, I began to wonder what kind of special magic each seemed to generate with people. It was more than just celebrity; they had an exuberance and delight that reflected on the faces of the people with whom they were talking. Everyone seemed to be having a good time. Looking back I think I was a touch jealous.

At about 2:00 A.M. I took my leave, and as I descended the front steps I heard the maestro call, "Wait!" Their car pulled up and the three of us got in. "Now where?" he said.

"To bed," replied Felicia, with some firmness, "at least for me." And she leaned her head back on the seat.

Turning to him I said, "Lenny, aren't you exhausted too?" It was the first time I'd used his nickname.

"I can't sleep, Schuy," he replied. "I never can sleep. Oh, God! How I wish I could sleep!" He looked driven and pale; and I was startled by this sudden change in mood. But it didn't last. He soon smiled broadly and suggested a nightcap. Of course, I accepted; I was delighted to win this sudden acceptance and intimacy. When we reached the hotel, and Felicia had gone to bed, he poured drinks and we settled down to talk.

And talk he did, fascinating talk on all kinds of subjects—politics, literature, theater, movies, and music, mostly music—he poured out his love for the art, his passion to share it. He explained his past relationship with Columbia Records and his desire for future recording freedom. He spoke about composing, about his enthusiasm for modern culture, about education, about his creative friends and his hopes for a better world. I grew excited—mesmerized might be a better word—by his prodigious ability to communicate; it was my first exposure to his talents as a teacher, which were just then reaching an ever-widening public through television.

It was, therefore, with quite a start that I suddenly noticed the sun beginning to edge in around the window curtains. I looked at my watch and realized we'd been talking for almost three hours. I rose and tried to thank him for an extraordinary time. He got up and gave me a big hug. "We're going to work wonderfully together!" And he walked me to the door.

Out in the corridor my head was swimming with the whole day and evening; I was exhilarated and exhausted. On reaching my room I collapsed on the bed, kicking off my shoes. I didn't even bother to take off my clothes. I just lay back on the pillow and was instantly asleep.

When I awoke it was past noon. The Bernsteins were due to leave Washington in just over an hour. I slapped some cold water on my face, brushed my teeth, peeled off my evening clothes, slipped into a fresh shirt, pants, and a jacket, combed my hair, and went down the hall to their suite. There the door was open, revealing what for all the world looked to be a levee. People were everywhere—sprawled on couches, draped over chairs, hanging off of table edges. The air with blue with smoke. In one corner, seated at a table having breakfast, was Felicia. For one wild moment I thought she was the Marschallin on the set for Act 1 of a modern-dress *Der Rosenkavalier*. "Hi there!" she said cheerfully. "Have some coffee." And she poured a cup.

"No, thank you," I replied. "I can't drink coffee in the morning. I like tea."

"Then we must order some straightaway!" Her hand went to the phone.

"Please!" I said. "Let me do that. You finish your breakfast." I reached for the phone.

29

"And while you're at it, order some bacon and eggs for me. I'm *starving!*" It was Lenny, making his entrance looking and sounding fresh and animated. His appearance started a veritable tidal wave of conversation. To each person in the room he seemed to give his undivided attention, including the waiter who brought his breakfast.

Presently people began drifting away, with hugs and kisses and exclamations of love; and the phone stopped ringing, and the smoke settled, and the bellboys came for the bags. And they were off on their way to that night's concert. I went to the lobby to say good-bye. They dazzled me. I hated to see them leave.

I returned to New York that afternoon and turned my attention to the maestro's contract, scheduling a meeting with his attorney-manager. I soon learned that because he found all business matters tedious, such discussions had to pass muster with three people—his secretary, Helen Coates; his accountant, Gordon Freeman; and the leader of the group, his spokesman and attorney-manager, Abraham Friedman.

At our first meeting, Friedman, a cross between an aging leprechaun and a balding Jewish Santa Claus, never lost his smile or his steel. He told me what was going to be acceptable: a twenty-year arrangement with minimum guarantees against maximum royalties and the right to record anything he pleased at any time he desired. There would be no more repertoire selection made solely by the company. He also made it clear that there were other companies prepared to meet these demands with even larger monetary guarantees than he was asking from us, and even one company—here the smile stretched all across his cherubic face—that was prepared to send a blank contract to be filled in as Bernstein desired.

I coolly replied that I didn't believe we would have any major problems. My heart was racing; I was playing everything by ear and really had no idea what my colleagues' reactions would be. I might be perceived as a brilliant negotiator, or an idiot. As I was reflecting on these feelings, Friedman gathered up his hat and briefcase and told me I had three days to make up my mind.

I immediately went to see Goddard Lieberson, my boss and president of the company, to report the discussion. "What do *you* want to do about these points?" he asked. "After all, you'll be responsible for carrying them out." Silence. I took a deep breath and said I wanted to proceed, that Bernstein, already a star, was positioned to become the most important musical figure in America, and we'd be crazy to let him go. Lieberson, his fingers tenting together as he spoke, agreed. "Our business-affairs people will give you a hard time," was his only comment. He knew I would learn a lot from the encounter. Anything involving Lenny was bound to be an interesting learning experience.

As it turned out, the business-affairs people and the company lawyers did kick up a fuss. They made it clear that they thought I was ruining Columbia Records by giving in to extravagant artistic demands. I sweated but stood my ground. Lieberson supported me; within the prescribed three days I was able to inform Friedman that we had a deal.

Next I had to settle the Philharmonic contract, not a challenging negotiation now that Bernstein was safely in place. Within a few more days I was able to ring Friedman again to tell him that this, too, was in order, and that we were now in business for many years to come.

My task after that was to establish the repertoire to be recorded during the first five years of this new arrangement. This meant organizing a planning meeting through Helen Coates, who watched over the maestro's schedule like a mother eagle. She had been one of his early piano teachers, the first to recognize that he was exploding with talent. A spinster, in the early 1940s she moved to New York to help with what Lenny always referred to as "the kitchen of life."

Miss Coates kept telling me how impossible his schedule was and that, in effect, I would have to stand in line. I told her that although she didn't know me yet, she would before we were finished, and that I hated long meetings and wanted to get on with the job.

The day finally came. Miss Coates ushered me into Bernstein's study at The Osborne, a turn-of-the-century apartment house across the street from Carnegie Hall. The building, with its long corridors, high ceilings, and wide spaces, had then, and still has, a curious, timeless feeling. The Bernsteins occupied a large, airy apartment on the fourth floor of the building; the maestro's study was on the second floor. Here a wide room had been fixed up to allow plenty of space for scores and books, a concert grand piano, a desk, sofas, and several comfortable chairs. Off to one side, with its separate door, was Miss Coates's office.

On Bernstein's arrival, Miss Coates took her leave, and he seated himself at his desk, pulling a yellow legal pad from a drawer, a pencil from a large glass jar, and reading glasses from his pocket. The maestro was tan, dressed in elegant, casual clothes, a small scarf around his neck. His face was relaxed, his hair loosely brushed. I noticed he was beginning to turn gray at the temples.

"Now that you've got the right to record anything you want, what do you want to start with?" I asked, to get the conversation rolling.

He fixed his eyes on me. "What I really want is to draw up a plan that will make us both happy. How's that for a start?"

"Couldn't be better from my standpoint," I said.

"Good," he replied. "We should begin with the Mahler symphonies. I plan to conduct all of them over the next few seasons and want to record them all. The public is ready for Mahler. His time has come."

He went on to outline his reasoning about this composer. As he did, his eyes took on a special light. Gone was the maestro-performer; I was now before the maestro-rabbi. He began telling me Mahler's life story. I was fascinated because many years earlier my feelings about this composer had been shaped by an old Victor Records catalog, the author of which had pontificated that there was not one crashing chord of Mahler that could equal a Beethoven cadence. As a consequence I avoided any of Mahler's music until my father-in-law introduced me to *Das Lied von der Erde*, and a friend to the First Symphony. After that I was hooked for life.

By the time the maestro-rabbi was finished, the maestro-performer began laying out a schedule that included not only the nine symphonies and the slow movement of the Tenth but also the song cycles. His plans were heady and exciting. At that time, the Bernstein catalog was extremely slim on basic orchestral repertoire, so we had plenty of room to maneuver Mahler in among the necessary Haydn, Mozart, Beethoven, Schubert, Schumann, and Brahms.

However, I left his study with several nagging problems that were not directly his concern. I had to cope with the other exclusive Columbia maestros, three of whom were extremely jealous of the public and corporate attention Bernstein was receiving: Eugene Ormandy, George Szell, and Bruno Walter.

Szell was relatively easy; we had a sister label, Epic, on which Szell and the Cleveland Orchestra were the undisputed stars. I needed to be very careful about

Ormandy and the Philadelphia Orchestra, however, as well as Bruno Walter and his Columbia Symphony, especially when it came to Mahler. Ormandy was already grumbling that Bernstein received all the repertoire plums. And Walter was Mahler's last living protégé: he had devoted a large part of his life to performing his master's music to often indifferent audiences; now, as an old man, he was hardly thrilled to see this relative youngster come to steal his thunder.

Walter was eager to record the First Symphony in the then new stereophonic sound. The First was also on Bernstein's list for early 1960; I would have scratched it but for the special repertoire clause in his contract. Since I really couldn't do that, I had to find a way to avoid insulting Walter, especially since it was his temporary illness in November 1943, while guest-conducting the New York Philharmonic, that had given Bernstein his first major career break. I decided to go ahead with both, reasoning this decision out with John McClure, who produced the Walter recordings in Los Angeles as well as the Bernstein sessions in New York.

In January 1960 McClure went west for Walter and a few weeks later appeared in my office carrying a set of acetate dubs made from the tapes. "You better listen to these," he said. "And you better be prepared." I put the records on my turntable and out poured the most unbelievably beautiful performance—measured, polished, serene yet robust and filled with passion—a reading of the work by a grand old master doing final homage to his idol.

After the symphony ended, I found it hard to move from my chair. I finally pulled myself together and knew I had to call Bernstein; contract or no contract, I had to ask him to cancel our plans.

When he finally came to the phone, I explained the situation, telling him that in my view this was Bruno Walter's finest as well as probably final Mahler statement and that we should postpone his recording of the piece to a later date. We talked for a few minutes, and finally he said: "Let me hear what you're raving about." I sent the dubs to him that afternoon.

A day later the phone rang. "Oh, my God," he said, "that's unbelievable! Forget about it from me. We'll do it at the end of the cycle. I couldn't bear the thought of trying to record the work now. It's *his*!" When I put down the phone, I realized that I had discovered a new facet of the Bernstein character: his collegial generosity, a trait he displayed throughout his career, although it was not always reciprocated.

Shortly after the Mahler episode we met again, this time in Carnegie Hall to discuss the *Faust* Symphony of Franz Liszt, a work he wanted to record and in which we had absolutely no interest. This was to be our first disagreement on a repertoire idea. He was determined to convince me that the work was a masterpiece badly misunderstood by the public; I wanted to assure him we'd lose our shirts trying to enlighten them.

We sat on the stage smoking cigarettes during a rehearsal break while, in his usual compelling way, he poured out the reasoning behind his choice. I was having none of it, refusing to be borne along by his eloquence. I pointed out that the work would be hideously expensive to record, would never sell enough to justify the cost, and, at least in my opinion, was not of such overwhelming importance as to require riding roughshod over business logic. The discussion ended with my agreeing to "think it over" as he went back to his rehearsal.

The next day I called to repeat that I felt it would not be a good idea. At this point he reiterated, very quietly, that he wanted to record it anyway and intended to do so under the terms of his new contract. A few hours later Lieberson called to ask me what was going on and why Bernstein was upset about doing something against our wishes. I explained the situation and he sounded sympathetic. "Well, let's hope he's right and you're wrong," was his only comment.

We did record the work, and very well, too, with the Philharmonic joined by the Chorale Arts Society and tenor Charles Bressler. The critics called it a "masterpiece long overdue in record catalogues" and praised Bernstein's interpretation as well as the foresightedness of Columbia. However, the album was a sales disaster. I wanted to forget it.

Later that year a package arrived at my office containing a picture of Lenny and me in earnest conversation—him pleading, me listening; it had been taken that day at Carnegie Hall as we had been discussing the Liszt project. It was a coda to the event, sort of a Bernstein apology.

During our years together he recorded some splendid performances—Eileen Farrell singing the *Wesendonck Lieder* and the *Götterdämmerung* Immolation Scene; Mahler's Third, Fourth, and Fifth Symphonies; Beethoven's First Piano Concerto with the maestro as both soloist and conductor; Ravel's *Schéhérazade* with Jennie Tourel; the Beethoven *Missa Solemnis*; the Bach Magnificat; all the Beethoven, Schumann, and Brahms symphonies; his own music for the film *On the Waterfront,* and a symphonic suite drawn from the songs and dances of *West Side Story.* We also did a remake, including all the dance music, of his score for *On the Town.* Betty Comden and Adolph Green, the show's authors as well as original performing stars, were on hand to re-create their roles, and, with Bernstein conducting, it turned out to be a lively package.

All this work was stimulating and exciting but by no means free from the bumps, lurches, and tensions that are part and parcel of life in the performing arts. Recording the *Waterfront* and *West Side Story* Suites, for example, brought a bucketload of problems.

Both of these pieces were orchestrated for the Philharmonic by Sid Ramin and Irwin Kostal as a surprise birthday present for the maestro; they were intended for live performances only. When he decided to record them, we had to pay both arrangers their original fees a second time, and this in itself was expensive.

The suites had their public debut at a special gala concert conducted by Lukas Foss. Bernstein was in the audience. The concert was splendid. Although I thought the recording a fine idea, I warned him to be careful about expensive recording-time rehearsals. "I know, I know," he said. "I know about expenses. Don't worry. I only need to touch up a few things before taping starts."

But I did worry; by this time I knew what Bernstein's idea of "touching up" meant. At every possible opportunity I reminded him that the whole project, while wonderful, was horribly expensive and entreated him please to be careful.

On the day of the recording, about halfway through the alloted time, I called McClure to ask how things were going. "Oh, just fine," he replied. "He's rehearsing away. But we haven't recorded a note yet."

"What?" I yelled, slamming down the phone and racing from my office to the studio.

I arrived as everyone was on a break, and sought out the maestro. "Listen," I said, "you promised me you only needed to touch things up and so far that's all you've done. I don't want to be difficult, but this recording could end up as the most expensive classical recording ever made, if you don't get on with it."

"Don't worry, dear Schuy," he said beguilingly, "it's going to be fine. You worry too much!" And he reached over and tousled my hair as he headed back to the podium.

The afternoon dragged on endlessly and the money kept being spent. It was too late to pull out; I had no choice but to complete all the work. When we finally finished, the disk ended up costing over $25,000 a side, something of a grim benchmark for the industry at the time.

Although it didn't help much, Bernstein was horrified when I told him and immediately offered to delay receiving royalties on this particular recording until the costs were recouped. I said I'd take him up on his offer if I needed to and suggested he pray.

He did, and so did I, and, miracle of miracles, by the end of 1962 all costs had been completely recovered and the record was making money for everyone. It still does, I'm happy to say, but I learned a permanent lesson about Leonard Bernstein: never accept the phrase "don't worry." Start worrying immediately.

The year 1962 shaped my relationship with Bernstein in other ways as well. We had been exploring how to adapt some of his television programs for adults in order to record them. He had a few ideas but needed time to think. "Why don't you come skiing with me at Aspen?" he asked one cold winter afternoon. "We can ski during the days and work at night." I thought this sounded fine, maybe even great, although I hadn't been on skis since I was a teenager. My wife, Betty, had misgivings. She looked worried. "Don't go," she said. "You'll break your leg."

I went anyway and everything was fine until our last day, when Lenny persuaded me to ski down the beginner's trail of Aspen Mountain while he went off with the experts. Norman Singer, head of the Aspen Institute, was appointed my skiing buddy and swore he knew a shortcut that would bring us down the slopes safely. He didn't. We got lost and ended up on the expert trail, where I watched in mounting horror as human cannonballs careened past us at God knows how many miles an hour. Between cannonballs we edged our way across the trail, gradually making a crisscrossed descent rather than a direct one at full speed. I was tense and terrified but kept going. Just as we were about to reach a rest plateau, I fell into a sitzmark (for you nonskiers, that's a hole left by some other skier who has fallen down) and felt something snap in my right leg. The ski patrol bundled me onto a toboggan and down the mountain we went, straight to the local hospital, where an X ray confirmed a painfully fractured kneecap.

Lenny was horrified—I'd told him Betty's prediction. "What are we going to do?" he asked. "She'll never forgive me for getting you into this."

"Don't be concerned," I replied magnanimously. I'm going to call her office early tomorrow morning." (She was assistant admissions director at New York's Dalton School.) "It will be OK. I'll tell her when her mind's on other things." And that's just what I did. After she realized that I was not marred for life, she said simply, but firmly, "Come home."

Lenny raced around finding wheelchairs and special crutches and people to help tuck me into cars, all the while feeling guilty and wondering what he was going to say to Betty. He chartered a small plane to fly us to Denver, where we connected with a flight bound for New York. When we arrived home he delivered me sheepishly to our front door, where Betty greeted us. She smiled at him. He seized on that as forgiveness, giving her a big Lenny hug.

During those often exciting years, the Chapins and the Bernsteins became good friends. Our relationship grew gradually, starting with after-concert supper parties where all kinds of people gathered for postmortems, or, more likely, discussions of theater and/or politics. Usually these parties lasted into the small hours, with people drifting out as their energies waned or morning appointments loomed too near. Occasionally Felicia would give up and retire herself, but not before seeing to all the details of the supper. We never stayed too long, at least not at first, because our four young boys, Henry, Ted,

Sam, and Miles, and Betty herself, always had to be ready for another day at the Dalton School.

The Bernstein children, then just Jamie and Alexander, were also at school, but Alexander was a frail youngster given to severe respiratory infections; there was much worry about his general health. Felicia talked to us about the problem as it became increasingly evident he needed to be in a warm climate. One winter she decided to withdraw him from school, first taking him to Arizona, where they stayed for several weeks. When the Arizona climate became colder than expected, she bundled him off to her family in Chile, sending him down to the South American summer under the care of Julia Vega, a soft-spoken Chilean who was then, and still is, the Bernstein family housekeeper.

When Alexander returned he was brown and healthy and had put on needed weight, but he had forgotten how to speak English. He had brought home with him a small crucifix in a box as a gift from one of his Chilean Roman Catholic relatives. Lenny paled at this and began introducing the boy to his Jewish faith. They had to talk together in Spanish until Alexander's English returned.

The relationship between mother, father, and children was always close, and another daughter, Nina, was born in 1962.

At the end of that year there was also another kind

of special—nonathletic—Bernstein-Chapin collaboration: Lenny had prepared a special narration for Benja-
min Britten's *Young Person's Guide to the Orchestra* to
use on one of his televised "Young People's Concerts."
At first he thought of his daughter Jamie to fill the role of
narrator but at the last minute changed his mind and,
knowing of our eldest son Henry's love for music and the
stage, offered the job to him. Henry was delighted and did
a splendid job, while I almost expired from nervousness
backstage. He also went on to record the work under the
maestro's baton.

Today, Henry is a teacher of music to small children
at the Nightingale-Bamford School in New York. Right
after Bernstein's death he showed the tape of this performance to illustrate the maestro's charisma, carefully
blocking out his name on the credits. At the end of the
show his pupils were moved and impressed, except for
one girl who raised her hand to ask who was that "nerdy
kid who spoke the words." He finally confessed and got
a round of applause.

During those busy years the Bernsteins would occasionally find the time to give a formal dinner party. One
such evening bears recalling because, besides being
funny, in a disastrous sort of way, it brought out the best
in all the assembled guests to prevent what might have
been a true social Armageddon.

In the early winter of 1963, Felicia decided to have
a small soiree to christen a newly designed dining room.

"And let's be formal," she said. "Black tie." We would be eighteen in all, mostly old friends of the Bernsteins and of ourselves.

The night of the party everything looked truly spectacular. For the occasion the living room was filled with beautiful flowers. The dining room, which had been fitted out with three tables, one for four people, one for six, and a third for eight, glistened with sparkling crystal and polished silver. The servants, Chilean every one, moved about efficiently in their formal black uniforms and white aprons. And as for the guests, I was convinced that we all seemed to glow in the candlelight, looking our collective best. It was a scene truly worthy of *Vogue* or *Town and Country*.

When dinner was announced I discovered I was seated at the table for four, with the great mezzo-soprano Jennie Tourel on my left, and Carmine Weissel, wife of the then assistant manager of the Philharmonic, on my right. Directly opposite me was Herman Shumlin, one of the most respected theater producer-directors of his time. As we sat down I introduced him to the two ladies, both of whom smiled vaguely but then began talking to each other. Herman looked at me and asked, in a stage whisper that could be heard across the room, who they were. I quickly told him, but he didn't seem the least interested or impressed.

As soon as we were seated Jennie turned to me and in her wonderful Russian-Paris-New York accent asked if I knew of her latest triumph in Chicago. I loved and admired Jennie Tourel, but she always seemed totally humorless, particularly when it came to her career, and consequently I replied very seriously that I did not. She then proceeded to tell the three of us all about it in some detail, enough even finally to catch Herman's attention, who would, every now and again, interject a sly comment.

The first course was a Chilean dish, *pastel de choclo*, a rich gummy stew with grated corn scattered throughout. We'd just been served when Herman, barely touching his plate or, as far as I could see, the table, overturned the whole thing into his lap. Plates and glasses of white wine began cascading toward him.

There were, of course, instant cries of consternation. We all tried to help, as Felicia rushed to his side. Fortunately, despite all the utensils, he escaped relatively unmarred. Julia quickly cleared and reset the table, and we recovered our collective composure and joined again in general conversation.

Soon plates were changed for the second course, a great roast of beef accompanied by a splendid burgundy. We all partook liberally (this was before all the anguished bombast about red meat and cholesterol), and I noticed Herman and Carmine Weissel enjoying each other's company. I, of course, was busy listening to the continuing triumphs of Jennie Tourel.

As we began eating I noticed Herman laughing gently at some remark of Carmine's, and as he did the table collapsed on him once again, this time even more violently. Everything—glasses full of red wine, cutlery, plates, even the dripping candlesticks—tumbled into his lap.

"What *is* this?" he asked in a deep, angry voice, rising slowly from his by now thoroughly splattered chair. He was covered with beef and wine and candle grease, to say nothing of previous traces of *pastel de choclo*.

This time Lenny and Felicia both hurried over in response to the anguished cries. Lenny, trying to clean off Herman's sleeves and failing in his efforts, knelt alongside Jennie and began picking up stray dishes and glassware. Jennie, totally ignoring the confusion and hardly breaking the rhythm of her conversation with me, turned toward him. "Lenushka," she said in a slightly peevish voice, "did you ever read my wonderful review from Chicago?" She launched once again into the account of her éclat, at the same time opening her evening bag to take out her *Chicago Tribune* notice. Clutching it in her hand, she began to read it aloud. In the meantime Herman, outraged, was dripping everything onto the rug, while Felicia was trying to persuade him to come away from the mess down to Lenny's dressing room, where, since they were more or less the same size, he could be outfitted in a complete change of clothes.

The other guests were trying to be sympathetic, most of whom knew something about Herman Shumlin that I did not: he had a fierce temper. Felicia, for one, knew it and was doing everything in her power to prevent an explosion, which, from the look on his face, was not too far away. She finally took his arm and led him gently but firmly out of the room. Meanwhile, as Lenny continued to pick up pieces of silver and glass, Jennie prattled on, regaling him with her succès fou.

Presently Herman returned; his pants had been sponged down and he was wearing a clean shirt, tie, and jacket. In his absence we found the problem with the table, a loose catch on one of the wings, and shifted the dangerous part to my area. With some suspicion and not a little hesitation, Herman sat down. We were all served again and ate well, even though Herman, understandably enough, never lost his somber and skeptical demeanor.

The next day Betty and I sent Felicia a plant with a card that read: "To Felicia Bernstein: The First Annual Herman Shumlin Award for Hostess of the Year." Herman, Lenny, Felicia, and all of us chuckled about this for some time afterward; Jennie, I later learned, finally did get Lenny to read her excellent Chicago review.

Shortly after this dinner, I decided to leave Columbia Records to accept an invitation from Lincoln Center to become vice president for programming. I didn't see much of Bernstein professionally until 1968, when, after ten years as music director of the New York Philharmonic, he decided to step down from the post in 1969, much to the sorrow of the Philharmonic trustees and the music public. He was appointed laureate conductor, a title especially created for him, and began making plans to compose and guest-conduct around the world. His departure, as it happened (another one of those curious coincidences), overlapped with the end of my contract at Lincoln Center.

Over dinner one night he broached the subject of our working together again. One of the ideas we discussed grew out of a suggestion made by his agent Robby Lantz about the future possibilities of music on television and the then brand-new concept of videocassettes.

Robby pointed out there was already a market for good music on television in Europe, but that apart from Bernstein's "Young People's Concerts" there was nothing comparable in America. He thought that there might be something we could do abroad to help solve this problem at home. Lantz recommended that, at the very least, all Lenny's future performances be recorded and filmed in anticipation of whatever new technological advances might be achieved in the communications world.

Somehow the idea of venturing into this area appealed to us both, as it did to his attorney-manager, his secretary, and his accountant. We formed Amberson Productions, a little production company to be attached to Amberson Enterprises, the organization that looked after his business affairs.

The name *Amberson* came, in part, from Lenny Amber, the name Bernstein used as a youngster in the popular music field. This, in turn, was derived from the

German word *Bernstein*, which translates into English as *amber*. This play with words was part of Bernstein's life-long fascination with games and puzzles, but the puzzle that faced us just then was to figure out what we could do with this medium. It was a challenge that, in a way, he had already met only a few years before, when he pioneered new methods of presenting music that had seized the public's imagination. This time we would try to capture the imaginations, and pocketbooks, of television executives across America.

THREE

The Teacher's Gift

O n 26 September 1985 the Museum of Radio and Television in New York mounted an exhibition and celebration honoring Leonard Bernstein's artistic contributions to television. It was a gala occasion on a very grand scale, opening with a black-tie dinner at the Library of the Hotel St. Regis and continuing for seven weeks at the Museum itself with special lectures and showings from Bernstein's video legacy.

I was one of the speakers at the dinner. I remember that, as I looked around the extremely crowded room, I kept thinking of the first time I had watched Bernstein on television. I had been bowled over by his explosive charisma and utterly captivated by his ability to share his enthusiasm for music. He had an unmistakable gift for teaching.

Fortunately for all of us, we now have the heritage of his kinescopes and videotapes, a cache that will be around to inspire and excite future generations.

It seems to me that the maestro's video performances can be pretty neatly divided into three distinct groupings: First there are the programs in which he acts as teacher/interlocutor, speaking on behalf of many different kinds of music—mainstream classical, contemporary classical, jazz, musical comedy, and rock. This category is represented by "Omnibus," "Lincoln Presents," "Ford Presents,"and the fifty-three remarkable programs that make up the acclaimed "Young People's Concerts." The second group would consist of the programs of his work as a composer, including his symphonies, some of his stage works—*Mass, Trouble in Tahiti, Wonderful Town,* and *Candide,* in particular—and his deeply moving *Chichester Psalms.* Finally there are the seventy-plus programs of his appearances as a conductor with orchestras such as the New York Philharmonic, the London Symphony, the Israel Philharmonic, and, especially, the Vienna Philharmonic.

Leonard Bernstein and I began working on television projects together in the late sixties and early seventies, but in order to understand the continuing impact he had on this medium one must begin with 14 November

1954, the day he made his television debut. The program was "Omnibus."

A word of history here: "Omnibus" began its life in 1952, created as the "TV/Radio Workshop" of the Ford Foundation. It was the first commercial television outlet for experimentation in the arts, and from the beginning the program's approach to music was fresh and unusual. For example, an early telecast featured selections from Mussorgsky's *Pictures at an Exhibition*, but instead of a traditional concert-style performance, the program enlisted the showman maestro Leopold Stokowski to explain the story behind the composition. Stokowski gave viewers a guided tour of a mock art gallery, pointing out the particular picture that inspired each musical section. The corresponding excerpts were played along the way, prompting the *New York Times* critic Howard Taubman to opine that "if the television audience must be led by the hand, it should get its verbal guidance at the beginning and the end, but once the composer has the floor he should be allowed to hold it." Never mind that one of the first programs didn't work quite as well as intended: it clearly demonstrated the determination of those involved with "Omnibus" to make the arts come alive on television.

The most slam-bang run of music programs in the series took off on the November afternoon that the thirty-five-year-old maestro discussed the structure of the first movement of Beethoven's Fifth Symphony.

From its opening moments it was obvious that a totally new approach to music and television was under way. Bernstein stood on a huge studio floor painted with the score of the first movement and pointed to the opening four notes with his right shoe. "Three Gs and an E-flat," he said, looking straight at the camera. "Baby simple."

During the half hour that followed, he took viewers on an intense and fascinating exploration of musical creation. He deployed instrumentalists as stand-ins for notation, alternating visual representations of Beethoven's first-, second-, and sometime later-generation thoughts about now-familiar passages with illustrations of their sound. It was both illuminating and amusing; the orchestra, unaccustomed to the glare of the camera's eye, sometimes looked like a bunch of embarrassed children caught playing hooky. Using the giant score as a backdrop, and with the camera looking down from a high angle, the musicians were arranged in positions that corresponded precisely with their instrument's notation in the score— the oboist seated above the oboe's musical part, the clarinetist above his part, and so on. All this was accompanied by the maestro displaying his unique gift for combining homely metaphors—the "last lap" of a symphonic movement—with nutshell lessons—"the artist will give away his life and energies to be sure that one note follows another with complete inevitability."

This first TV appearance inaugurated a revolutionary era in music telecasting. The maestro brought to the medium much more than his boundless enthusiasm and natural gifts: he knew how to convey the intellectual and emotional passion of his art in a way that was accessible and stimulating to all types of viewers. His style at once confronted the middlebrow on his or her own level, without stooping; you might say he seduced his viewers along the paths of least resistance. More than any other musician before—or since—Bernstein understood television's potential to unlock the mysteries of music and make the home audiences care as deeply as he did about the glories of its expressive language.

A year later, another "Omnibus" appearance confirmed his status as one of the medium's "great communicators." This time, in a sequence entitled "The World of Jazz," he applied his skills to explaining the intricacies of the *St. Louis Blues*. With slides, piano demonstrations, and a jazz quintet to support his points, he again revealed his special knack for making musical discussions vivid and fun. Even if viewers couldn't completely grasp all his examples of harmony and minor-scale developments, it was easy to be carried along by his charm and infectious enthusiasm.

"The World of Jazz" was followed in late 1955 by "The Art of Conducting," a program in which he discussed the importance of the conductor and illustrated what might happen if an orchestra worked without a leader. A year later he explored "The American Musical Comedy," tracing its history back to *The Black Crook* of

1866, Gilbert and Sullivan, and Victor Herbert, discussing its roots in vaudeville and variety shows. Carol Burnett was one of his assisting artists on that program and did a splendidly wicked imitation of Ethel Merman in *DuBarry Was a Lady* as well as sing excerpts from *South Pacific*.

One of my personal favorites was the program that aired on 31 March 1957. On this occasion Bernstein set out to demolish the widely held notion that the music of Johann Sebastian Bach is boring. He plunged right in by declaring that when he was a young piano student he was taken by the "immediacy" of the slow movement of Bach's *Italian* Concerto and proceeded to illustrate his point. He conceded that much of Bach can come across as "more motion than emotion," which perhaps accounted for the difficulty comtemporary audiences, accustomed to music of dramatic contrast, had in responding to it. He characterized Bach's music as being "about one thing at a time, just as the architecture of a bridge grows inevitably out of one initial arch." Then he went on to talk about Bach's musical structures as basically a single theme or idea followed by elaboration, discussion, reiteration, and argumentation. "That frightening bugaboo counterpoint," he said, "is nothing to be afraid of"; and he illustrated from scores, showing how the contrapuntal strands of Bach's chorale preludes resemble "smoothly flowing rivers dotted with islands" of chorale tunes. A choir, dressed to suggest the church-going fashion of the composer's time, as well as a troupe of instrumentalists, aided in his remarkable effort to get beneath the skin of Bach's scores.

All told, the maestro's contribution to the "Omnibus" series consisted of twelve appearances covering specific topics and fifteen non-"Omnibus" specials, including travels with the New York Philharmonic to Tokyo, Moscow, Berlin, Tel Aviv, Venice, and London, and studies in the musical anatomy of Stravinsky's *Oedipus Rex*, Bizet's *Carmen*, and Puccini's *La Bohème*.

Starting in 1957, however, CBS decided to feature Bernstein's talents on a more regular basis by televising the New York Philharmonic's Young People's Concerts. The concerts themselves were a Philharmonic tradition; I can remember as a child sailing paper airplanes around Carnegie Hall during long and frequently boring presentations of various kinds. But in Bernstein's hands, the concerts had become the perfect forum to showcase his flair for instruction and inspiration. Yet the question of how to transform those live music events into interesting television remained.

Enter Roger Englander, a young musician and stage director who had worked with the maestro at Tanglewood eleven years earlier. They had become good friends, even at one point discussing a collaborative adaptation of a James M. Cain novel for what would have been Bernstein's first opera. When that project evaporated, Englander moved on to television, where he became a CBS staff producer-director assigned to news, sports, and public affairs. At heart, though, he was still a musician, and as such deeply concerned about finding more television commitment to good music, especially for young people. Richard Lewine, director of Special Programs for the network at the time, suggested he might be just the person to work with Bernstein. It was an association that went on to create what is now recognized as television's greatest contribution to music and arts education.

The format devised by Bernstein and Englander began with the first broadcast on 18 January 1958. Recognizing that few people could match Bernstein's attention-holding powers, Englander knew it was equally important to use the medium's unique resources to enhance and underscore each concert's primary themes. Not only was the camera work carefully planned in advance to coordinate with the music being played but special visual material was inserted to illustrate key points. Pictures of composers appeared at the mention of their names; so did views of rocket ships when they were needed to demonstrate the propulsion of, say, a Rossini overture. In this way the Young People's telecasts combined the best features of a live concert program—the excitement of musicians performing before a large audience—with technical feats more often associated with studio productions.

Bernstein's magical rapport with the audience at Carnegie Hall, and later at Lincoln Center's Avery Fisher Hall, and his fervent discussion of the first concert's topic—"What Does Music Mean?"—came across so effectively that two more Young People's broadcasts aired in the months that followed. Their success, in turn, persuaded CBS to keep the series going. Subsequent concerts were aired live on those Saturday mornings when the concerts took place.

They probably would have continued indefinitely as live presentations tucked safely away in broadcast limbo had it not been for the famous 1961 Newton N. Minow speech voicing public sentiment about the blandness of network programming. Minow, chairman of the Federal Communications Commission at that time, lashed out at network television, calling it, among other things, "a vast wasteland." CBS countered his stinging indictment by scheduling the "Young People's Concerts" at 7:30 P.M. on Saturday nights, virtually prime time. They stayed in that slot for three seasons, until the FCC went on to other campaigns, taking the pressure off. They were then transferred to Sunday afternoons, and many of the new viewers followed.

By this time, the "Young People's Concerts" had become a part of pop culture. They were parodied on nighttime comedies; cartoons appeared in magazines; and there were references to Beethoven and Bernstein in *Peanuts*. Films of the concerts themselves were loaned to schools; two volumes of Bernstein scripts were published by Simon and Schuster; and the shows were translated into twelve languages for syndication in forty countries.

Englander has described the process by which each program came to fruition. Bernstein usually planned the subjects in such a way as to incorporate music he was rehearsing for the Philharmonic's regular subscription series. Weeks before the concert date he would send a draft of his script, handwritten in pencil on legal pads, ready for typing. "The script conferences were happily anticipated rituals held at Bertstein's apartment," Englander noted.

> Our staff was small, but boisterous and creative. Mary Rodgers, with her experience in writing children's books, would suggest ways to clarify and simplify the text; young John Corigliano [later composer of *The Ghosts of Versailles*] would advance musicological arguments befitting a budding composer; Ann Blumenthal, stopwatch in hand, would time Bernstein script-reading and piano snippets, miraculously allowing for the badinage of crosstalk and peppery asides; Jack Gottlieb would meticulously catalog the musical examples for the orchestra's cue sheet; and Candy Finkler would document the word changes in the script, and insist that we maintain some level of decorum.

Englander records that Bernstein always wrote every word of each script, inviting suggestions and comments along the way, but insisting that he would not be comfortable delivering someone else's words. "On the other hand," Englander noted, "he left the visual side of the productions completely to us."

And that visual side was really the orchestral score. It became the shooting script, with the music holding the answers to the director's task of translating sound into pictures. Englander explains: "As in all temporal forms, the individual shots were important only in context: changing the image at the correct musical moment was more important than the content of the picture itself." These methods did not pass unnoticed. In an early review Howard Taubman noted that "the exceptionally good camera work of the television crew appeared as if it were part of the orchestrations themselves."

During the early years of the "Young People's Concerts," Bernstein was also, occasionally, invited to return to the more adult-oriented format he had pioneered with "Omnibus." On a late Sunday afternoon in November 1958, in a slot usually reserved for Ted Mack's "Original Amateur Hour," the maestro, assisted by the New York Philharmonic, offered another of his ebullient lecture/ demonstrations, this time on the final movement of Beethoven's Ninth Symphony. The program opened with the maestro, seated in what appeared to be his office, grabbing the score, looking directly into the camera, and exclaiming, "What a phenomenal work! There's so much in this work!" He then embarked on an enthusiastic discussion, punctuated by assorted examples at the piano, and once again uncovered the wonders of musical structure in a way that helped even inexperienced listeners to come to terms with Beethoven's formal powers.

This time Taubman wrote: "Bernstein has the gift of making music fascinating. His talks are knowledgeable, witty, serious and ingeniously threaded with musical illustrations. . . . As an intelligent musician he never loses sight of the fundamental nature of the art he is analyzing. As a performer who rejoices in the pleasure that flows from a responsive audience, he has mastered the knack of throwing light on the processes of music in an exciting way. He knows the uses of legitimate showmanship; he can illuminate his subject without patronizing or demeaning it."

After the performance of the "Ode to Joy," with the Westminster Choir and soloists Leontyne Price, Maureen Forrester, Léopold Simoneau, and Norman Scott, the program concluded as it had begun, showing Bernstein back in his office, calmly smoking a cigarette. The camera revealed the toll of conducting—it was apparent in his sloped shoulders and now more relaxed manner. But with the graciousness of a host at the end of a long, tiring party, he thanked the audience for watching. The intimacy of television made a small moment like this irresistible.

The Maestro and the Cathedral

1969, as I've already noted, was the year Bernstein stepped down as the Philharmonic's musical director, but he continued to lead the "Young People's Concerts" until 1972. Meanwhile our little production company was ready to begin its independent life, although having, as yet, nothing specific on its agenda.

This state of affairs did not last long. One night, over a drink, Lenny casually mentioned a telephone conversation he'd had that day with William S. Paley, chairman and founder of CBS, during the course of which he'd asked what CBS was planning to do about the 1970 Beethoven Bicentenary. Paley replied that he didn't know and asked if Bernstein had any ideas. The maestro did, of course, but told Paley only that he would get back to him.

"What do you think?" he asked me.

No fool, I immediately replied, "What kind of a show do *you* have in mind?"

"I don't have all the ideas," he murmured, "but if we do a show, *Fidelio* must be featured. I'm conducting it at the Theater an der Wien, where Beethoven composed the work and conducted the premiere. We must get this on film. It's an opera that can be wonderful, thrilling, and deeply moving, if it's done right."

I had no argument on that point, remembering Bruno Walter's marvelous performances at the Metropolitan Opera. But I did not think a film on Beethoven could be built just around *Fidelio*. "Who should we think about to direct the film and work with us?" I asked.

"I like Humphrey Burton's work," came Lenny's reply. "Do you know him?"

I'd never met Burton, but I knew a lot about him from artists who thought his music productions on the BBC and London Weekend Television were the best around. "No, I don't," I replied, "but perhaps I should see if he can fly over and talk to us."

Within a couple of days Burton arrived in New York, and he, Lenny, and I, sometimes joined by Lenny's agent Robby Lantz, began discussing general ideas. In the middle of one such conference, Burton suddenly asked if we had any plans to televise or tape the maestro's scheduled performances of the Verdi Requiem in London's Albert Hall that February. Finding there were none, Burton exclaimed, "Oh, with this new production company we should make a videocassette of your performance, not in Albert Hall but in St. Paul's Cathedral. Can you imagine a more glorious setting?"

Burton's question had the effect of suddenly showing me my top production priority: to see if I could organize financing for such a project.

I went to Roger L. Stevens and Robert Whitehead, the original producers of *West Side Story*, and told them what we had in mind. "Who's singing in the Requiem?" Stevens asked.

"Arroyo, Veasey, Corelli, and Ruggero Raimondi," I replied.

"That's good enough for me," he said. "How much will it cost?"

I'd worked with Humphrey to develop a budget and promptly replied, "Between eighty-five and ninety thousand dollars."

He thought for a moment. "You have a deal," he said. "Any film with Bernstein, the Requiem, St. Paul's Cathedral, and such a cast is bound to work!" He took a piece of paper and began roughing out an agreement, which he gave to me. I went over it with Lantz, and two days later we all gathered in Lantz's office to sign. The entire contract amounted to a page and a half of text, clear in language and intent. Stevens signed, I signed, Bernstein signed; and we were off and running with our first production.

While we were developing these plans, I began my Beethoven assault on CBS. I called Mike Dann, who was then senior vice president for television programming. Dann had an impressive track record at CBS and was clever enough to have survived the political vagaries of several different administrations. We had known each other since the late 1940s, and I'd watched his career with interest. I knew him well enough to know he harbored secret dreams of becoming an impresario of music, opera, theater, and dance. I thought we might have a chance of organizing a Beethoven celebration if we could spark his interest in it.

Dann was interested. He told me he'd just sent Howard Taubman, recently retired from the *New York Times*, to Vienna to try to work out a program with the Vienna Philharmonic and the Vienna State Opera. He said he'd just about settled on a telecast of the Ninth Symphony from the opera house. I told him that wasn't big enough. "Bernstein is conducting *Fidelio* and a series of concerts with the Vienna Philharmonic to celebrate this event in a major way," I said. "We want to develop a special program that would be a grand television overview of Beethoven's life." Dann asked who would be working with us, and I mentioned Humphrey Burton, who had just returned to England after our initial set of collective discussions.

66

"Call him," Mike said in his best baronial manner, pointing to the telephone on his desk. "Get him over here today!"

Fortunately I reached Humphrey at home. Explaining that I was calling from Mike Dann's office, I asked if he could possibly return to New York immediately. He caught the urgency in my voice and quickly agreed to be on the next plane.

Within twenty-four hours, a somewhat travel-worn Humphrey and I sat down with Dann and members of his staff to outline a program that would include scenes from *Fidelio*, the last movement of the Ninth Symphony, a movement of the First Piano Concerto, which Lenny was playing and conducting at the Musikverein, and biographical material. Dann listened attentively, finally answering us in a manner reminiscent of Louis B. Mayer, David Belasco, and Sol Hurok all rolled into one. "Fly to Vienna immediately," he said, "and see what you can put together!"

Pausing only long enough for Humphrey to catch a little sleep and me to pack a bag, we flew to Vienna and began a round of exhausting talks.

On arrival we discovered that the maestro's *Fidelio* production was to be the centerpiece of the 1970 Vienna Festwochen. That meant dealing with Ulrich Baumgartner, the festival director, as well as the orchestra committee of the Vienna Philharmonic, the intendant of the Vienna State Opera, the Opera's chorus

representatives, plus countless officials of Austrian State
Television.

The Viennese are charming people, their city is a
delight, but they have their own particular way of doing
business. We sat in meeting after meeting where, after
lengthy exchanges, just as we would begin to think that
we'd arrived at various understandings, the rug would be
pulled out from under us. I usually summed up our discussions by putting the key points into a memo for all to
initial, which we would all proceed to do. But, invariably,
just as we were actually saying good-bye, someone was
bound to call out, "Oh, Mr. Chapin. What a pity! Please
forgive me, I don't know what I was thinking about. Of
course you cannot do that on Thursday. And Friday is
impossible, too!" We would all return to our seats; the
problem usually turned out to be money. We would shake
our heads apologetically, trying to match them in polite-
ness, but eventually, we'd have to agree to give them at
least part of what they suddenly discovered they needed.
Sometimes these "codas" took place on the street outside
the building we'd just been in, as we were getting into a
taxi. Sometimes we'd have them in the lobby of the Hotel
Sacher, where we were staying. One actually occurred at
the airport, as we were literally standing at the departure
gate. Humphrey and I both quickly learned that whatever
contract we'd agreed upon was certain to be changed and
that we'd better be prepared for it.

Basically, however, we accomplished a great deal in a very short time (about thirty-six hours), and I was able to return to New York with enough information to put together a pretty secure budget. I completed this, together with an outline of the show, and took the papers over to Mike Dann's office. I told him I was leaving for England on our Requiem project in exactly ten days and asked if CBS could possibly decide yes or no before that time. I also made sure to remind him of the initial conversation between Paley and Bernstein.

The next days were filled with working out the details for the Requiem. I had a hunch Franco Corelli might cancel at the last moment—he is famous for doing this—and I wanted to protect us by lining up another world-class tenor. I sought out Placido Domingo, whom Julius Rudel had discovered in Israel and brought to the New York City Opera. Almost immediately the Metropolitan signed him as well, and he was enjoying a huge success, although he was by no means the superstar he is today. That year he'd replaced Corelli at the openings of La Scala and Covent Garden. He was becoming known as a stand-in; naturally this was beginning to rankle. Who would be pleased with such a label?

Domingo was in the middle of his Metropolitan season. I asked him, together with his wife and concert manager, to tea at the Plaza Hotel and explained our problem. I could see his sensitive eyes react with sadness when he heard the name Corelli. "Listen, Mr. Domingo," I said, "I believe in telling the truth. I think Corelli will back out of this and I think the film and recording will be yours. At this stage in your career, it would not hurt you to be associated with Bernstein."

"Oh, no, of course not!" he rejoined. "Nothing would please me more. I have such admiration for the maestro!" And he smiled in a way that left no doubt in my mind that he meant exactly what he said. "It's just I don't want to stand by for Corelli anymore." I said I understood his point and asked if there wasn't a way we could work out an arrangement that did not put him in a compromising position. We finally agreed that I would call him from London at 5:00 P.M., New York time, on the Friday before his Saturday Metropolitan broadcast and two full days before our filming was scheduled to begin. He would come if we asked him.

His agent and I reached agreement on his fee and, almost as an afterthought, I asked whether he'd be in Europe in April when, if the Beethoven project went forward, we might be filming the Ninth Symphony. As it happened he was free, and I offered him a contract on his own. This pleased him very much.

The day for our departure to London neared and still there was no word from CBS. I kept calling Dann and his deputy Jim Krayer, but nothing was happening. I finally talked it out with Krayer, and we agreed that Bernstein should speak to Paley once more.

I broached the subject with the maestro; he glared at me. "You know I *hate* doing that," he said. "I will never sell myself. It's like begging. I won't do it." I explained he didn't have to do anything in bad taste and suggested that he simply call Paley on some friendly pretext and close out the conversation with a casual reference to the fact that "his people had submitted a Beethoven proposal to your people." He scowled at the idea but did it, albeit reluctantly. Paley said he'd have a look.

And have a look he did, because within a couple of days Dann called with the news that we had a deal, subject to the completion of a contract and an acceptable final budget. I turned everything over to Abe Friedman, asking him to keep in touch, and flew off to London with Felicia and Lenny and Oliver Smith, who was to be my Requiem coproducer and designer.

The morning after our arrival Humphrey greeted me with the news that the British musician's union would not agree to a contract including videocassette rights, an arrangement that was supposed to have been settled by the management of the London Symphony. While I was pondering this particular setback, Oliver made it clear that lighting St. Paul's was going to be a major problem in itself; he was going to need every yard of electric cable and every klieg light in London that was not being used in the West End. "I'm going to cost a lot of money," he whispered in my ear as we entered the cathedral, "but it will be beautiful. When I was an architecture student I studied this building inside and out. I know every inch of it. See up there?" he pointed to the arches in the transept. I looked, but saw nothing other than the arches themselves. "There are beautiful frescoes hidden under that dirt. We're going to light them. That's going to take a lot of expensive candlepower."

"Go ahead," I said, feeling a little like someone approaching quicksand, "we're in this together." He patted me on the back.

From the cathedral I returned to the Savoy Hotel, where I'd set up a production office. We had a lot of work ahead; we were scheduled to shoot the film in less than a week and once under way we had to complete the project in one night. Ordinarily this would have been a bad joke, but filming was to be preceded by numerous musical rehearsals and a Sunday night performance in Albert Hall. A separate recording was also being made by Columbia Records.

Arrangements for all the film production services were part of a deal Humphrey and I made with London Weekend Television, from whom we received both equipment and a fee for the exclusive use of the program in Britain. Now that officials of the London Symphony had failed to solve the videocassette problem, I decided to plead for help from London Weekend's management.

Their labor experts reminded me that because the cassette idea was just coming into focus no union wanted to set precedents in this tricky new world. I reported that

I'd managed to obtain these rights from all the solo artists involved as well as the chorus; only the orchestra was not cooperating.

Presently I was joined by Vic Gardiner, a George Smiley type from London Weekend's legal office. He didn't say much as we raced around London in a continuingly futile effort, but at the insistence of Oliver Smith we at least did all our traveling in a hired car with driver. Although it had required me to thrust aside my normal New England thrift—I rarely spent money on such frivolities—Oliver gave me good advice: the car and driver saved a lot of time and energy.

Despite all our efforts, however, the problem remained unresolved. Finally, on the third morning, our London Weekend friend went off alone. By lunchtime he returned with a look of grand satisfaction. He'd made an agreement with the union. It was clearly understood that our contract was not setting any precedents and that other projects of this nature would have to be arranged on an individual basis, but we could proceed with our plans.

When I asked how he'd accomplished such a miracle, he just smiled. All these years I've been waiting for some strange body to be exhumed form Westminster or Knightsbridge. So far all is quiet.

The afternoon of this victory I returned to the Savoy for a cup of tea with Felicia. As we sat together in her small sitting room, I heard the most pitiful bleating coming from next door. It was obviously the Verdi score, but the singer sounded as if he'd swallowed a peach pit and was about to leap out the window. I looked at her questioningly and she shrugged. "It's been going on all afternoon," she said. "It's Corelli. He doesn't feel well." I listened for a moment, then buried my head in my teacup.

Presently the maestro entered and poured himself a cup. "Did you hear that?" he said, looking sad and concerned.

"I did," I replied, "and I think we're going to have to do something about it."

"We'll wait until after tonight's piano rehearsal and see," he replied, "but we better be ready with Placido just in case."

At the rehearsal, with all the soloists and the chorus present, it was obvious Corelli was not himself. He was pale, perspiring, and terrified. During a break, Humphrey, Lenny, and I all agreed he had to go. I excused myself and went tearing back to the hotel to keep my telephone rendezvous with Domingo. He agreed to fly to London immediately after his Metropolitan matinee.

Now I had to figure out how to fire Corelli and find a replacement tenor for the Albert Hall concert (Domingo would only arrive in time for the recording and filming). I decided to sleep on the problem.

The next morning I was awakened very early by the phone ringing in my ear. It was Loretta Corelli, Franco's wife, hysterical and crying, telling me her husband was sick and had to cancel the whole Requiem package. I sat bolt upright in bed. "You mean he's canceling everything now?" I asked.

"Si, Signor Chapin, everything. We go back to Italy. Franco has such beautiful memories of the *Cavalleria Rusticana* with the maestro." (Corelli had sung *Cavalleria* with Bernstein earlier that season at the Metropolitan.) "He don't want anything to disturb this." More sobs. "Good-bye," she said, and hung up.

My first reaction was relief. With his withdrawal we had no obligations to pay off his contract and I could save money. But then I thought about Sunday and Albert Hall. It was, after all, Saturday morning, and this did not leave much time to find a substitute. I began calling various agents but it seemed that every tenor was either out of town or singing that night. Finally, when I was approaching desperation, I lucked out with Robert Tear: he knew the part and was available to rehearse Saturday night and sing the next day. He was superb. Just as a precaution I found out that he was available and willing to undertake our film if Domingo fell ill.

Following the Sunday performance, rehearsals began again for the film and recording. Our soloists, now joined by Domingo, were understandably anxious, guarding themselves carefully since they were required to sing steadily over the next few days. Only Ruggero Raimondi seemed truly unperturbed. After every session he would leave either Albert Hall, where the recording was taking place, or St. Paul's Cathedral looking impassive, a differ-

ent beautiful girl on his arm each time. When he returned
for the next session, he was always calm and satisfied.
Martina Arroyo, not known for her robust health, stood
up wonderfully well too, as did the mezzo, Josephine
Veasey. As for Domingo, he was having a great time. It
was a happy quartet.

Our real problem was time. On the day of our filming we were allowed into the cathedral early for technical
preparation but couldn't begin actual rehearsals until
noon. The filming itself was to start at 7:30 P.M. before
an invited audience; that audience began assembling in
the early afternoon. By 5:00 P.M. the crowds were standing in double queues before the doors. This sea of humanity lent an air of anticipatory tension to our efforts.

I arrived at 8:00 A.M. and watched as electricians
crawled all over the ceiling installing lights. What seemed
like endless rolls of cable were playing out and disap-
pearing into the vastness. Eight cameras were being stra-
tegically placed around the chancel, the nave, the great
choir, and the transept; carpenters were putting finishing
touches on the orchestra platform and covering the sides
and floor.

In the middle of the chaos stood Oliver Smith, overcoat draped around his shoulders, looking like a battle-
field general whose troops are advancing against heavy
fire. Humphrey Burton was there as well. Usually unflap-
pable, this morning he looked a little harassed. "I'm having camera problems," he said as I approached. "One is

dead and another is dying. I've sent for replacements but I don't think we can find them. We may have to make do with six." He smiled wanly.

Just then I was approached by the verger. "I beg your pardon, Mr. Chapin," he said, pronouncing my name "Shypin," as is frequently the case in England. "Could you have a word with the dean?"

"Certainly," I said, and went along after him.

The dean greeted me with a certain reserve. I took a moment to thank him for all the cooperation we were receiving and assure him he would not be displeased with the results. He smiled coldly. "At the moment, our problem is that there has been *smoking* in the cathedral. This must stop or we may be forced to cancel the entire performance." I immediately thought of Bernstein, who was always smoking; with the extra tension of these sessions he would go crazy without tobacco. "I don't wish to be difficult," the dean went on, "but there are other than purely ecclesiastical reasons for this, particularly fire prevention. We must enforce the rule without exception." I told him I would pass the word and again thanked him for his help. He thawed a little, enough for me to bring up his participation in what we planned for an opening: a procession down the nave with the soloists walking two by two and Bernstein accompanied by the dean in full clerical regalia. Things warmed considerably once I made this suggestion, but there was no question about the smoking prohibition.

At noon the musical forces arrived. The maestro was taken into a small office that was to serve as his dressing room and command headquarters. It was a round, damp room with a small w.c. and wash basin located far up a dark, frigid spiral staircase. There was an electric heater near the desk. Opening one of the several mystery doors in the rear curve of the room I discovered a passage leading to additional stairs that evidently led to the roof. Out there the wind was whistling: it was cold.

I stepped back into the office just as Lenny was lighting a cigarette. "Hold it," I said, walking forward to take it away from him. "We can't smoke anywhere in the cathedral. I've been told this in no uncertain terms. Unless we all behave, the whole project will be canceled."

"But what am I going to *do*?" he wailed.

"I think I've found a solution," I said in a calm, authoritative voice. "Put on your overcoat and follow me."

I led him to my newly discovered staircase passage. It seemed even colder this time, but the wind did carry the smoke away. He lit a new cigarette. "God, it's cold here," he said. "Is this all you can do?"

"You want to try the roof itself?" I asked. "Maybe we can get a safety belt and strap you to a gargoyle up there."

"Very funny, you're very funny," he commented as he took a last puff. "You're supposed to be my friend." His teeth chattered as he smiled.

The full rehearsal with all cameras and lights began at 4:00 P.M. Humphrey had preplanned his camera shots for musical aspects and Oliver had blanketed the cathedral with sufficient light to catch the subtlest carvings and colors. All that remained was to assure good sound.

We were recording the sound track in stereo, but since at that time the majority of television sets were still monaural, we had to try to create the illusion of antiphonal sound; actually it was a question of producing a picture on the screen that seduced the viewer into thinking the sound was omnipresent. One big problem was stationing the trumpets for the "Dies irae"; another was spacing the timpani and brass in order not to blanket the strings, woodwinds, and chorus; still another was overcoming cathedral echo. As the afternoon wore on I began to think we'd never get things ready.

But, somehow, all the experts involved managed to arrange everything; the filming would begin almost exactly on time. Every available inch of the cathedral was filled by an eager audience; there was an air of high expectancy. As Humphrey called for "action," the soloists, preceded by the verger and followed by Bernstein and the dean, began their stately procession toward the podium. I crossed my fingers and, even as a longtime Unitarian, looked beseechingly toward the high altar.

All thing considered, the performance proceeded quite smoothly. The antiphonal trumpets sounded fine, the chorus and soloists were in good voice, and the orchestra was on its toes. However, two terrible musical bloopers occurred and would have to be corrected. One was the unison entrance of the soprano and mezzo in the "Angus Dei," a section that always causes trouble; the other was Arroyo's opening phrase in the "Libera me," punctuated, as it was, by the cathedral chimes ringing out ten o'clock. Also, I sensed that Humphrey was having trouble with his cameras. I went around to the various monitors and, although all was quiet, I was aware of tension.

At this point there was nothing I could do. I walked around to the front of the cathedral. The look down the nave was deeply moving—the orchestra, the chorus, and the soloists all bathed in light; the ceiling, the transept, the great choir, and the chancel all aglow. Even the audience was luminous. It gave one the feeling of being in another world.

Finally, a little after 11:00 P.M., the work was concluded. The same group of verger, soloists, dean, and conductor walked solemnly back to the vestries. Once there the soloists peeled off to the exhibit hall, which was being used as their dressing room, and the maestro and clergy went into the little round office.

After the artists had left the stage, Humphrey came out to announce that the necessary retakes would begin in about thirty minutes. He and I then joined the maestro.

Lenny was sitting huddled at a table, an overcoat hugging his shoulders, two heavy bath towels around his neck; he was sweating hard, his hair matted against his forehead. He had the score in front of him and was busy marking places that needed to be done over. The verger and dean stood off to the side, watching in awe as people came and went with cups of tea, books of music, light lines, and other impedimenta of television filming. When Humphrey and I stepped into the room, Lenny grabbed both of us. "We have *lots* of problems," he said. "We should really do the whole piece over."

Humphrey spoke quietly and assured him that that was not the case. He pulled out notes and the two began making a list of retakes deemed imperative. Lenny was obviously dying for a cigarette; he kept looking over at me and the cathedral officials. "I'd give *anything* for a cigarette," he finally moaned loudly, "anything."

The dean looked at me, then at the verger, and approached the table. "Mr. Bernstein," he began, "after the unbelievable beauty you've given us tonight, something I'll never forget as long as I live, please, smoke as much as you want!" Then he reached through his cassock into his pants pocket and took out a lighter. Lenny leapt for his cigarettes and was soon puffing away to his heart's content. There were many problems with the film still to be faced before the night was over, but at least the performance itself had reached out and touched the Church of England.

The retakes went slowly. Everyone was tired and, as the tension of the performance itself wore off, more mistakes were made; the more errors, the more irritated everyone became. Roger Stevens and Bob Whitehead had flown over from New York and were now sitting in the audience looking at their watches. We had organized a supper party at the Savoy for the key people on the project. I knew we were running later than expected and that this was adding to the costs.

But there was no hurrying Lenny. We made retake after retake, culminating, as far as I was concerned, with the third try at the "Libera me." By the time the cameras rolled for this one, Martina Arroyo was bathed in perspiration from the hot lights and general fatigue. As she started singing "Libera me, Domine, de morta aeterna," two rivulets of sweat ran down her cheeks. I stared at a monitor; she looked to be weeping. Fortunately her musical performance matched the image on the screen; Hollywood couldn't have done it better.

Finally, at about 1:30 A.M., we were finished. Surprisingly, hardly any of the audience had left; I took this to be a good omen. We arrived at our party shortly after 2:00 A.M. to find a room full of sleepy waiters and subdued, exhausted guests. My optimism began to fade, but Lenny was full of energy. His table was the only lively spot in the room.

I had a drink and a sandwich with Oliver, Roger, and Bob and made a date with Humphrey to look at our tapes at 9:30 that same morning. As I said good night, Humphrey looked worried. "I really don't know what we have," he said, "but we might as well see." With a slightly sinking heart, I asked Roger and Bob to join us.

Barely seven hours later we all squeezed into a small screening room at a Dean Street studio. Bernstein was not there; I had persuaded him to stay away, knowing that we would apprise him of the problems soon enough. The room was packed: Roger and Bob both came with their wives, and Humphrey had brought his future wife as well as a couple of other people involved with the production. Oliver and I, sitting together, were both disquieted by Humphrey's obvious nervousness. It suddenly occurred to me there was a distinct possibility that Amberson Production's first independent project might end up a total disaster, but I kept this ghastly possibility to myself. Then the lights lowered.

The raw master tape of the performance came on the screen. As the opening titles rolled, I surreptitiously glanced around the room and saw Humphrey scrunched way down, his eyes barely visible over the seat in front of him. Stevens and Whitehead were both sitting up straight. Oliver was slumped alongside me. The others were watching in a noncommittal way.

But soon we were all captivated by the dignified and moving procession to the podium; Lenny's simple bow to the dean just before raising his hands to begin; the lowering of lights in the cathedral as the quiet opening strains of "Requiem aeternam dona eis, Domine" floated upward; the lights coming up again with "Te decet hymnus, Deus, in Sion"; the blaze of wrath in the harsh open-ing chords of the "Dies irae."

As the tape moved along we were gripped by the power and beauty of the work and of the setting in which it was being performed. The four soloists were inspired; the cathedral fairly breathed with the piece. At those moments when the musical intensity became almost too much, the cameras would break away for a glance at a statue or a look at a ceiling fresco. Every work of art shown matched the spirit and mood of this Verdi master-piece. The whole performance seemed gloriously impro-vised on the spot.

I was deeply moved. Tears came to my eyes, partly from the emotion of the performance and partly from relief: for we clearly had something priceless before us. I reached into my pocket for a handkerchief; as I did, Oli-ver asked if I had another. I found an extra and gave it to him. He blew his nose. Soon a hand tapped me on the shoulder. I raised my right arm, and the handkerchief was plucked from my hand. Humphrey slid over and asked to borrow one. I suddenly realized that everyone in the room was weeping, and that I seemed to be the only one with handkerchiefs. Eventually someone slipped out and returned with a package of tissues. It was passed around as the rest of the performance unfolded before us.

When it was over the lights went on, but at first no one spoke. Finally Oliver rose and turned to Humphrey and me. "I think this is the proudest moment of my professional life," he said, hugging us both at almost the same time. Humphrey dissolved. In a quiet voice he explained that when he had left the party he was absolutely certain he had failed. Bob Whitehead and Roger Stevens, tears coming down their cheeks, felt every penny invested was worth it. I sat silently, overcome.

There was a lot of work to be done on the tapes—inserting retakes, balancing sound, finding a few better shots—before we would be ready to show anything to the maestro, but it was obvious we had the material.

I went in search of a telephone to call Lenny. I tried to tell him how moving it was, and how very pleased he would be. My voice cracked in the process. Words failed; I could only hope that somehow he *knew*. And he did.

The Birthday of Music

With the completion of the Requiem, we could now turn all our attention to the Beethoven project. Lenny flew off to Paris for two weeks of concerts, while I returned to New York for final contract talks with CBS. On arrival, I found that Abe Friedman had this matter well in hand, so well, in fact, that Betty and I decided to pop off for a few days of sun in Jamaica. We were guests of Mary and Hank Guettel. One of the high points of the visit for me was settling the final details on the telephone with CBS while standing waist deep in an elegant swimming pool.

After Jamaica I went directly to Vienna, checking

into the Hotel Sacher, where I caught up with Lenny and Humphrey. The three of us settled down to discuss exactly what we wanted to include in the unusual television production, well aware that we had a rare American network commitment: a ninety-minute prime-time special on an artistic subject.

We felt, and I articulated this point perhaps more than the rest, that we had to produce a program honoring Beethoven in a manner authentic to music lovers and scholars and yet accessible to the general public who might, after seeing the broadcast, be curious enough to explore his life and music further. What we needed was a 1970s version of "Omnibus."

Lenny was particularly concerned about *Fidelio*. He believed that Beethoven's creative genius was wrapped up in this, his only opera and that the Festwochen production should be our focal point. Humphrey and I agreed about its importance but were not certain how to handle it on television, since opera and the tube was a conundrum each of us had wrestled with in our respective countries without much success.

A few historical notes on this subject: Back in the 1950s the National Broadcasting Company began exploring ways of bringing these two art forms together, investing considerable money to create the NBC Opera Company. This group made innovative strides, coming up with brisk English translations and casting young, attractive singers who were also good actors. They supplemented these television efforts by sending the company on two national tours, both of which I supervised. The tour repertoire included *Le nozze di Figaro*, *Madama Butterfly*, and *La Traviata*, all three of which were considered among the most successful television performances.

The telecasts themselves were, in fact, passable; but the two tours were sensational. Obviously the former helped build an audience for the latter, perhaps in giving a teasing flavor of each masterpiece.

Essentially the same problems remain in force today: trying to jam full-scale opera productions onto an essentially postage-stamp television screen already marred by indifferent sound systems. These problems are curiously exacerbated by the Metropolitan Opera telecasts, which range from spectacular productions to intimate operas, all of which look very much alike on the screen. These telecasts will undoubtedly continue as long as Texaco wishes to foot the bills, but, unfortunately, straight-out opera productions are basically just not compatible with television.

Back in 1970, however, opera films were deemed to be one of the answers to world television's growing cultural needs. They were being made by the gross throughout Eastern and Western Europe and were uniformly terrible. We didn't want to head into the same morass with *Fidelio*.

After a lot of discussion we ended by agreeing to a format that divided our program into three parts: a biography of Beethoven built around Bernstein's performance of the First Piano Concerto; rehearsal and performance excerpts from *Fidelio*; and the last movement of the Ninth Symphony. Lenny began working on the script and Humphrey started scouting locations. I chased around Vienna completing contract assignments.

The first order of business was to establish command headquarters at the Sacher, where the maestro was staying and where the concierge and staff were in awe of him and ready to bend over backward to help.

It should be noted here that by the time of this particular project, Bernstein was already larger than life to the Viennese, and not merely as a musician. He was something of a folk hero, a dashing figure representing the energy and drive of America. When he appeared on the streets, he invariably drew a crowd of people asking for his autograph or just standing back and applauding. It was all extremely heady. I felt, somehow, that his unique position was bound to be helpful in accomplishing the slippery tasks ahead.

I set about calling upon the Vienna Philharmonic, the Vienna State Opera, the Festwochen, the opera chorus representatives, the various theater unions—stagehands, wardrobe, makeup—the management of the Theater an der Wien, the Ministry of Education and Culture, the directors of Austrian Radio and Television (who were our copartners in this venture), and officials at the Schoeller Bank. These were the major organizations that had agreed in principle to participate during Humphrey's and my earlier rush through the city in January. But our oral and memo understandings now had to be translated into contracts. With the Viennese, this turned out to be a constant lesson in elusiveness.

Early one morning, for example, after filming was already under way and contracts seemed to be settled, my room phone rang, awakening me out of a sound and sorely needed sleep. It was the concierge, bearing the news that representatives from the orchestra, the opera chorus, and the Festwochen had all arrived unexpectedly to see me.

"I know, Herr Chapin, they have no appointments, but there seem to be certain difficulties. I'll put the orchestra in the Blue Room, the chorus in the Coffee Room, and the Festwochen in the Red Room. Shall I notify the maestro and Herr Burton?"

"Yes on Herr Burton," I replied, "absolutely no on the maestro." The idea of Lenny dealing with any of this rigmarole was too much. The "kitchen of life" was bad enough; I could just imagine what he would think about what was obviously going to be an unexpected banquet hall of problems.

Humphrey joined me in the lobby and we started with the chorus. Simply put, they wanted more money than agreed to in their contract and more guaranteed payments in the event of reruns, all matters we had thrashed out in long meetings before. Humphrey glared at them and finally brought his hand down sharply, making a fearful racket as he hit the top of the table around which we were sitting. "No more!" he shouted. "No more. Do you hear?" He became very red in the face. We hadn't discussed strategy and I was surprised at this uncharacteristic outburst. The chorus leader looked startled. Humphrey went on. "You think just because this project is CBS in America and involves Maestro Bernstein there's a bottomless well. Well, there isn't, and if you want to work with us, fine. If not, stop wasting all of our time." He picked up his coffee cup, took a sip, and banged it down into the saucer. I caught the message and added that I, too, was ashamed and shocked by their inability to stick to a signed agreement.

The chorus representatives conferred among themselves in German, occasionally glancing over at Humphrey and me. The leader finally turned and said, "You take care of us if the film is shown in theaters. You make a formula. Then we agree to everything. We'll sign new papers right now."

"I've heard all this before," I said, rising to the moment. "How do we know you won't find more difficulties?"

"You have our word for this," the leader replied, looking very solemn. Humphrey and I exchanged glances. I went on, "We'll have these points put on paper. You return here tomorrow morning at 8:30 A.M. to sign." They bowed, bade us auf Wiedersehen, and left. We moved on to the Festwochen in the Red Room.

Here I knew we were going to face an extremely touchy matter. The day before, in some preliminary background filming at the Theater an der Wien, the house curtain had been lowered too close to one of our lights and a section of it caught fire. Lenny was rehearsing the overture at the time and kept right on while stagehands shouted, "Feuere!" and brass-hatted Viennese firemen clomped around the stage. A fire extinguisher was sprayed over the offending section and the flames quickly disappeared. Some orchestra members tried to peek over the pit to see what was happening, but Lenny brought them back to order and continued his rehearsal.

As it happened, the cameras were turning during all this commotion; and later we incorporated the scene into the final version of the film to illustrate the show-must-go-on spirit of an opera house. But, of course, we had no idea of doing this at the moment of our confrontation with an angry Herr Ulrich Baumgartner, the festival director.

"There will be no more filming at the Theater an der Wien," he stated, with special emphasis on the words *no more*. "You are causing too much trouble. It's all *unmöglich*. I'm ordering your cameras and crew out of the building."

It would, indeed, have been "impossible" to leave the theater at this point and Baumgartner knew it. He was putting on a good show for his companions, two swarthy gentlemen who turned out to be festival officials in the Viennese city bureaucracy. They nodded in vigorous agreement at his comments.

I explained that the accident had not been our fault, although we were nonetheless deeply sorry it happened. I reminded the three of them that a theater stagehand had made the mistake, bringing down the curtain at the wrong moment, and stated that it was not fair to turn us out for something we did not do. I spoke in my skimpy German, throwing in English words when I couldn't think of anything else.

We continued to talk for some little time. Finally Baumgartner agreed that if we could regain permission from the theater management itself, we might continue what we already had under way. We shook hands on this and I assured him, and the two officials, that his name and that of the Vienna Festwochen would appear prominently on the screen both in Austria and in the United States.

Leaving Humphrey to cope with whatever problems the orchestra representatives had brought to the Blue Room, I went straight to the Theater an der Wien to see if we could placate the management. I was greeted with stony silence and negative looks. There were four or five people at the meeting, and we were obviously getting nowhere. Finally I asked to speak to the manager alone.

"We must agree to let you continue," he said the minute the room cleared, "but my colleagues, well, they feel perhaps you might do something to help us over all the, shall I say, strain of these last days?" I reminded him it was his stagehand who had made the mistake. He merely shrugged and looked helpless. "Well," he said after a pause, "let us say the accident wouldn't have happened if your special lights had not been there."

I looked at him long and hard, struggling with my temper. "I'll consult our lawyer," I finally said. "He'll be in touch with you." We shook hands. Later we made a handsome monetary donation toward the upkeep of the building.

However, despite these—and other—difficulties we did move energetically ahead, filming the seventy-one apartments Beethoven lived in during his thirty years in Vienna, the rehearsal room and stage rehearsals of *Fidelio*, the First Piano Concerto with Lenny playing and conducting the Vienna Philharmonic in the Musikverein, and the orchestra performing the full Ninth Symphony in Vienna's other big music hall, the Konzerthaus. We took aerial shots of the city and the surrounding countryside, expecially those woods and parks where Beethoven walked. We absorbed and filmed as much as we could in order to have plenty of raw material for shaping our final version.

Spring blended into early summer, and 1970 marked a particularly lovely summer in that area of the world. Lenny had left the Hotel Sacher and was living in Grinzing, a smart suburb of Vienna, in a house belonging to Herbert von Karajan's first wife. The house had a lovely pool and garden; when the sun poured in the whole place glowed, giving a feeling of what the Vienna woods must have been like at the turn of the century.

On days between filming, visitors came and went in steady streams, seeking out the maestro for projects around the world. One was Wolfgang Wagner, the director of the Bayreuth Festival, who arrived all ruffles and flourishes, bent on persuading him to conduct *Tristan und Isolde* in 1972. Lenny had been a friend of Wolfgang's younger brother, Wieland, who until his death was the postwar artistic conscience of the Festival. Both brothers bore a striking resemblance to the photographs, statues, and portraits of their grandfather, Richard.

Wolfgang spoke in a tight, controlled voice about what a joy it would be for Bayreuth if Bernstein were to come. As he talked he seemed to be having some kind of problem with his right hand: it kept slowly moving up from the arm of his chair. As subtly as possible he moved his left hand over to control it. At first I thought this was some kind of subconscious nervousness; I glanced over at Lenny to find his eyes riveted to the same phenomenon. It suddenly struck me we'd seen it before in Stanley Kubrick's *Dr. Strangelove.*

Lenny was polite; he promised Wolfgang that he would think over his suggestion. We drank some wine together. Later, in discussing the visit, Lenny decided he would feel uncomfortable working at the Wagner shrine, even though he was conducting freely in both Austria and Germany. "Maybe later on," he said, "but the time is not right."

Elliott Kastner and Topol came, the former a movie producer and the latter a popular Israeli actor complete with masculine energy, sex appeal, humor, and almost overwhelming charm. They wanted Lenny to compose and conduct for a new film. Franco Zeffirelli also turned up with a film project, *Brother Sun, Sister Moon,* for which he wanted a Bernstein score. Unlike Kastner and Topol, Zeffirelli followed up his visit by sending deputations of acolytes—writers, designers, assistant directors—to keep up a relentless attack.

The pressure never let up. Massimo Bogianckino, then director of La Scala, arrived, and we walked together one overcast afternoon in the Schönbrunn gardens. He wanted Lenny to return to La Scala, where, in the mid-fifties as the first American conductor in La Scala's history, he garnered great triumphs with Maria Callas in productions of *Medea* and *La Sonnambula.* "Anything he wants," Massimo stressed, "anything he likes. He must come back. The public demands it!"

UNICEF sent a representative in the person of Leon Davico to arrange for a huge benefit concert with the Vienna Philharmonic. "Only Bernstein can do it," Davico pleaded. Marcel Prawy, the Viennese musicologist and artistic director of the Volksoper, always wanted to discuss revivals of Lenny's shows and talk endlessly about ideas for new ones; Peter Weiser, director of the Konzerthaus, was constantly begging for "ten minutes"; Rudolf Gamsjaeger, manager of the Musikverein, wanted new commitments; Reif-Gintel, intendant of the Staatsoper, pressed various ideas, as did representatives from the Ministry of Education and Culture, from the Foreign Office, even from Bruno Kreisky, the chancellor himself, who was an old friend of Bernstein's.

One visitor was always welcome—Princess Lily Schoenburg. Beautiful, bright, and funny, she would often whisk Lenny and me away to her family castle, a mid-eighteenth–early-nineteenth-century pile on the Rainergasse. The castle was nestled in the Schoenburg family private park and was, quite literally, falling down. It was presided over by the Gräfin Schoenburg, Lily's mother, who herself was a grand holdover from the Austro-Hungarian empire.

Lily and her mother lived alone and were virtually penniless; whatever they could scrape together went to patch the roof. Lily was the last in her family and was, at the time, unmarried, because there was no proper young Austrian (read: Hapsburg) prince to be found. Music was her solace and passion; she was an accomplished pianist. She and Lenny would play together, often for the Gräfin and myself, but occasionally for charity with members of the Vienna Philharmonic in charming chamber-music concerts. On these occasions, usually held in the late afternoon, the music would be followed by candlelight suppers served on tables spread over the castle lawn. The effect was fin-de-siècle Vienna right out of the storybooks.

Others who were always welcome were the Schoeller family, the late Fritz von Schoeller, his late wife, and their then small children. Fritz ran the Schoeller Bank, one of the last private family banking houses in the city. He was an elegant Austrian aristocrat who had first met Lenny and Felicia in 1966 when the maestro conducted *Falstaff* at the Opera.

Once, during a winter break in our schedule, he invited Lenny to come skiing with his family in San Anton. Arrangements were made for the maestro to take the evening train into the Austrian mountains. He would stay at the same hotel as the Schoellers, ski and socialize with them, and return to Vienna five days later. During his absence we planned to shoot scenes and backgrounds that did not require his presence, and also to take a closer look at the footage we already had. Lenny promised to let me know on what train he'd return, but by the morning of the fifth day there was no word whatever.

At about noon I called the hotel in San Anton and was informed that he'd left early that morning and was flying back. Indeed he was: he arrived at the Sacher at about 4:00 P.M., after a nearly five-hour trip in a chartered helicopter. He looked fit and rested, reporting that the train had been a rough-and-tumble affair that had made it impossible to sleep and that he had determined to avoid a repeat. My New England background came to the fore. "Chartered a helicopter?" I asked. "How much did it cost?"

He looked at me. "I've no idea. I didn't ask."

He gave me the charter papers and I went to the phone. When I reached someone in the company who spoke English I asked about the charter. "Ah yes," said the voice, "Maestro Bernstein this morning from San Anton. Wonderful! A great honor for us!"

"To be sure," I said, "but how much is all this going to cost?"

"Let's see," came the reply, "San Anton to Vienna and back to San Anton again. That's almost ten hours flying for the machine and ten hours for the pilot."

"They usually go together," I commented.

"Oh, yes, of course," he murmured, "but it does add to the expense. Let's see . . . I must check again with San Anton, but I think our bill will be in the area of five thousand dollars." I thanked him, hung up, and reached for the nearest chair.

I must have paled considerably because Lenny was by my side in an instant. "How much was it?" he asked, with a slight catch in his throat.

"Five thousand dollars, at least," I replied.

"My God!" he exclaimed, "Five thousand dollars! I had no idea." Now it was his turn to pale. "What are we going to do?"

"Pay it," I said. "I'll have a check for them in the morning." Then an idea dawned. "By the way, you didn't by any chance think about Beethoven while careening down those slopes?"

"Yes, I did," came the reply. "I even wrote some script." He went to his briefcase and took out a large pile of yellow legal-size papers.

He *had* been working. The material was rich in descriptions and outlines of Beethoveniana, including a first draft for the crucial denouement of our film.

"With this, I think we can put the helicopter down as a production expense. I don't know whether CBS will accept it, but it's certainly worth a try."

He looked a little relieved. "Well," he said, "that's your decision. But I promise the next time I'll ask the price first!"

A few days later Fritz Schoeller's secretary called on me to formally present a few additional bills in connection with the maestro's trip. I paid them immediately, as they all seemed in order, but was amused at the precision with which they were ticked off—so much for the train ticket, so much for laundry, so much for skis, so much for steambaths. Schoeller wasn't a banker for nothing.

Not too long after this adventure, the Schoellers invited both Lenny and myself for a weekend at Reichenau, the country seat of the Schoeller family some fifty miles south of Vienna.

Reichenau is a comfortable hunting lodge, with streams, pools, gardens, and incredible walks and drives. Fritz was responsible for thousands of acres of mountains and valleys. The house itself was pure Hapsburg: stuffed stag heads, roebuck, deer, and antelope stared down from the walls, antlers gleaming. We were surrounded as well by stuffed birds and fish, interspersed with pictures of hunters and fishermen with their catches, each outfitted in lederhosen, feathered cap, and loden coat. My bedroom was large and comfortable, with a high ceiling, a fireplace glowing with a low fire, a nightstand with basin and bowl, and puffy eiderdown quilts. The windows looked out over the mountains, and on the first night I flung them open to breathe the fresh, vigorous mountain air. I remember falling asleep instantly, and later found that Lenny the insomniac had as well, at least judging from his enthusiastic report at breakfast the next morning.

Some weeks later, when Betty joined me for a brief visit, we were both asked to Reichenau, and I was able to show her some of its beauties.

The Schoellers and Lily Schoenburg were wonderful divertissements, but our task was to concentrate on Beethoven and we were rarely away from this. By mid-April we had filmed pretty much everything we wanted except *Fidelio*. After long conferences we decided to film the entire dress rehearsal from start to finish and cover the actual opening night only if we ran into disaster.

101

For the dress rehearsal we asked the Festival and Opera authorities to request that the audience come in evening dress. They were delighted to cooperate and sent word that no one would be admitted who was not in formal attire. We stationed people outside the theater doors to tell the audience that they were going to be photographed and turn away any that didn't like the idea. Since the rehearsal was by invitation only, no one refused; a Bernstein rehearsal was a big enough event in itself, but when it was also the dress rehearsal for the official opening of the Beethoven bicentenary season it had an extra dimension.

At 8:00 P.M. we started. From the moment Lenny entered the pit it was obvious that this was going to be a very special night. Tensions normally present at dress rehearsals were there, of course, but tempered by something else—a kind of special eagerness. By this time our technical people knew the theater well; Humphrey knew exactly what he wanted. We were as prepared as we could be; the rest was up to the artists. And did they ever come through.

By the end of the opera, as the chorus rang out "Heil sei dem Tag, heil sei der Stunde," it was obvious we had captured a rare performance. The backstage cameras took over to cover the curtain calls, and as they did chorus members were seen embracing each other, stagehands shaking hands, and the maestro, clothes soaking, was seen gently chastising Gwyneth Jones, the Leonora, for not watching him carefully enough. They went out to bow together and the house rose. The ovation was overwhelming, a powerful experience for everyone. I breathed a sigh of relief. We had a fine performance, even though, as yet, no specific ideas as to how we were going to use it.

There remained one more segment to film before the maestro's camera chores were finished and he could take off for Israel while Humphrey and I assembled the show from the miles of material on hand. None of us was completely satisfied with the draft denouement he had sketched out while skiiing in San Anton. We had planned it to be a spoken essay—Bernstein one-on-one with his public, talking about Beethoven the artist and the man— to be presented just before he conducted the last movement of the Ninth Symphony.

A crew was assembled to film this segment at his house in Grinzing. Even as we started, it was clear that the script was not yet right. After a couple of takes he called a halt and, gathering up his legal pad and pencils, ran upstairs to his bedroom, closing the door firmly behind him.

About an hour later he reemerged, handing me his script. As I read what he'd written I realized it was brilliant, giving just the right mood and thrust to our entire project. Humphrey agreed.

The cameras, reset for a new take, rolled on Lenny, seated at the piano, looking at a Beethoven score and then, unforgettably, speaking to the television audience:

> Well, for the better part of three months now I've been living in terms of Beethoven, thinking about his life, visiting his houses, reading his letters, but most of all living with his music. I've studied it, and restudied it, rehearsed and performed it over and over again, and I may report that I've never tired of it for a single moment. The music remains endlessly satisfying, interesting, and moving, and has remained so for almost two centuries and to all kinds of people. In other words, this music is not only infinitely durable but perhaps the closest music has ever come to universality. That dubious cliché about music being the universal language almost comes true with Beethoven. No composer ever lived who speaks so directly to so many people, young and old, educated and ignorant, amateur and professional, sophisticated, naive, and to all these people, of all classes, nationalities, and racial backgrounds, this music speaks a universality of thought, of human brotherhood, freedom, and love.
>
> In this Ninth Symphony, for example, where Beethoven has set Schiller's "Ode to Joy" in the finale, the music goes so far beyond the poem. It gives far greater dimension and vital energy and artistic sparks to these quaint old lines of Schiller: *Alle Menschen werden Brüder*—all men become brothers; *Seid umschlungen Millionen*—Oh, ye millions embrace ye; *Ahnest du den Schöpfer, Welt?*—O world, do you sense your creator? In other

104

words, this music succeeds even with those people for whom organized religion fails because it conveys a spirit of godhead and sublimity in the freest and least doctrinaire way, which was typical of Beethoven. It has a purity and directness of communication which never becomes banal. It's accessible without being ordinary. This is the magic that no amount of talk can explain. But perhaps there was, in Beethoven the man, a child inside that never grew up and to the end of his life remained a creature of grace and innocence and trust even in his moments of greatest despair. And that innocent spirit speaks to us of hope and future and immortality, and it's for that reason that we love his music now more than ever before.

In this time of world agony and hopelessness and helplessness we love his music and we need it. As despairing as we may be we cannot listen to this Ninth Symphony without emerging from it changed, enriched, encouraged. And to the man who could give the world so precious a gift as this, no honor can be too great and no celebration joyful enough. It's almost like celebrating the birthday of music itself.

When he finished, and the cameras were off, we all burst into spontaneous applause. We broke out a bottle of champagne to toast the maestro and acknowledge that the principal photography for "Beethoven's Birthday" was now completed.

Within the next few days Lenny flew off for concerts in Israel while Humphrey and I settled down to look at our reams of tape and film. Our partners in the venture,

Austrian State Television, were eager to know how we were coming along and were not the least bit shy about expressing their opinions. I was mostly concerned about American audiences, who were to be given a serious program in prime time, something almost unseen and unheard of during a normal broadcast year. CBS was already making noises about ratings, although to be fair they realized from the beginning that what we were doing was a loss leader. From their standpoint, the program would certainly be broadcast in as harmless a moment as possible in the prime-time schedule.

After a few days with the Austrian technicians, two things became obvious: we were not getting good results from their film and tape laboratories and we were no further along in resolving our most perplexing problem— what to do with *Fidelio*. Humphrey and I argued back and forth but came to no conclusions. Finally we decided to postpone any decision on this matter in favor of completing the first part of the program, a pictorial and narrative biography of Beethoven.

Here we were in total agreement. We would use part of the First Piano Concerto as a musical bridge to take viewers on a tour of Beethoven's Vienna, its parks and woods and streets, showing them drawings and caricatures of the period along the way that visually portrayed various phases of his life. Then, after changing from the Concerto to the relentless rhythms of the second movement of the Ninth Symphony, we would demonstrate his restlessness through brief glimpses of some of the seventy-one apartments in the thirty-seven houses in which he lived.

When completed the effect turned out to be galvanizing: in a matter of just over twelve minutes, the viewer gets both a feeling about Beethoven the man and a tantalizing sense of Beethoven the genius.

With this and the full last movement of the Ninth Symphony we had a brilliant beginning and ending to the program but no acceptable middle section. *Fidelio* was not only a weight around our necks but a serious stumbling block to producing a good film. We needed outside help and we needed it fast. We also realized we weren't going to find it in Austria; London, with the English film industry within easy reach, seemed our best bet. Humphrey had thought of a specific editor we might turn to.

"You'll like Michael Bradsell, you'll see," he said. "He's quiet and imaginative and mad about music. He also edits Ken Russell's films."

"Let's meet him," I replied, "He sounds made for us. We haven't all that much time left to find a solution."

A few days later Michael joined us in a London screening room. A short, roly-poly man with sprouting red hair and a fierce beard, he looked like a mad prophet from the Old Testament as he sat gazing at the *Fidelio* material on the screen, no expression whatever on his face. After about thirty minutes he said he'd seen enough. We stopped the film and brought up the lights. He looked at both of us, still expressionless, and in a barely audible voice told us that he thought he might have a few ideas. He asked to take our material for a couple of days, saying that he'd let us know when he was ready for us to reconvene.

I went off to visit English friends, and exactly forty-eight hours later Humphrey called with the news that Michael was ready. We reassembled in the same screening room; Humphrey and I both a little frazzled.

"Are you ready?" Michael asked considerately. We nodded; the lights went down.

Onto the screen came film of Bernstein rehearsing the principals in a Theater an der Wien rehearsal room. The atmosphere is light and cheery but thoroughly professional. We see him talking about *Fidelio* to his cast, explaining how this tempo should move and that rhythm be accented. He speaks about the black and white characters of the piece, either all good or all bad, and how they must be rendered more human and less like the cardboard figures they are in the libretto. He devotes a lot of attention to Theo Adam, the Pizarro of the production, explaining to him how to his thinking Pizarro has the worst time of all because he is so relentlessly villainous. He must be given some human qualities, show some sign that he is a disturbed man. Adam listens patiently to these comments, the camera catching the interplay between the two of them.

Next we see a stage rehearsal with piano: Bernstein and Otto Schenck, the director, are talking about the Pizarro problem. Bernstein is explaining his theories and Schenck listens, nodding in agreement. "Let's have him wear spectacles to read the message about Don Fernando's arrival," says Bernstein.

"Wunderbar!" exclaims Schenck and, going up on stage, he takes off his own glasses and hands them to Adam.

"And be paranoid!" exclaims Bernstein. "Otto, he should tug at his collar; he should sweat with fear and look around to see if his weaknesses are observed."

"Right, right!" says Schenck, and in German and pantomime he shows Adam what he wants. Adam shakes his head and in German says that he's played this role all over the world and never before has he been asked to do things like this.

"He's afraid he'll mar his good looks!" exclaims Bernstein, and laughs. The camera catches Bernstein and Schenck watching Adam rehearsing the new business.

The next shot is of Adam in actual performance, putting on glasses and tugging at his collar. The effect is powerful. The audience has seen the evolution of a dramatic idea from conception through rehearsal to the final result.

"I've looked through all your material and you've enough to carry this idea through the whole production,"

Michael commented as the houselights came up. "The segment will be about the making of *Fidelio* and not just use *Fidelio* itself." Humphrey and I shake hands; we know we're in business.

Over the next weeks Humphrey worked with Bradsell to assemble a rough cut of the entire show while I returned to New York to attend to other Bernstein business. We agreed to meet again with the maestro in New York right after the July Fourth holiday to complete the project.

When the three of us did meet again, New York was in the middle of a stinking summer heat wave. Temperatures hovered around the mid-nineties during the day and never got below the high eighties at night; the humidity was brutal. We gathered in a midtown editing room; the air-conditioning clanked ominously while we showed Lenny what we still needed from him—the final narration for part one and the bridging sequences for *Fidelio*. As we were spreading out our materials all over the room, the air conditioner shuddered and stopped.

It was 9:00 P.M. There was little chance of finding another room at that hour. The only thing we could do was strip down to our underwear, drink endless glasses of iced tea, wrap our heads in towels, and hope for the best.

At around 1:00 A.M. Lenny tore up all the script he'd written and flung it against the wall. "Not good, not good," he murmured impatiently. "Let's look at the opening again." The images flickered across the editing screen. He said nothing, just stared while biting his lower lip.

Humphrey sat back, a hand across his forehead, his glasses fogged in the hot dampness. I sat looking at them both, remembering India and the jungles of Burma in World War II. The silence and the heat and humidity were inhuman. Finally Lenny looked up. "I've got an idea," he said. "Go away for half an hour and let me think it out." He turned his back to us and began writing.

We returned a half hour later to find Lenny looking as if he'd just conducted a full program. He was sweating from every pore but didn't seem to notice. "Let's look again," he said, "and I'll read what I've done here and see how it times out with the film. See what you both think."

The machine began and he, with one eye glued to the screen and the other on his script, read through a narrative giving the salient points of Beethoven's life with passion, humor, and directness. He'd found the key.

It was now 3:00 A.M. "You guys look tired," he said. "Go home. I'll finish up the *Fidelio* bridges." Humphrey insisted on staying; but I took him up on his invitation and returned to my apartment, where I dozed in air-conditioned comfort until around 8:00 A.M. When I got back to the editing room, Lenny looked much the same as when I'd left, though Humphrey looked blue with fatigue. As I walked in Lenny shouted, "We've got it! Let's show him!"

The machine whirled again. Bernstein's voice sang out with his words, and the musical clues were clearly indicated, both for the beginning of the show and the connecting material for *Fidelio*.

Indeed, they did have it. From that night and morning in the hot-box to the final product itself very little changed. The three parts were spliced together accompanied by all the connecting narratives, the music was edited, the color balanced, the titles added, and three weeks ahead of schedule I called the CBS television people to invite them to a screening of their program.

They came. Lenny, Humphrey, and I each spoke briefly, then we screened the program. When it was over, the executives shook our hands. "We'll win an Emmy with this," Mike Dann remarked. "It's beautiful. Thank you."

We were all encouraged. A few days later I gave the final print to CBS, returning $2,500 of their money that we hadn't used (and don't think *that* didn't cause eyebrows to go up!) but was informed that the program would not air until 1971, missing the Beethoven bicentenary by a whole year.

The program was aired in England and throughout Europe, of course, at the right time, but not in the United States. *Sic transit gloria*: culture on commercial television.

Never mind. It collected world prizes, including a 1971 Emmy. Two of its three parts, the Piano Concerto and the Ninth Symphony, were recorded in their entirety and now have separate lives as performance videos. The *Fidelio* material is used in music schools to introduce students to the work. All of the material reflects the musical and personal energy of Leonard Bernstein at a prime moment in his career. And fortunately for all of us, that moment is timeless.

"I Want to Do Anything I Can Do to Help"

I n the summer of 1970, Bernstein was invited to tour Japan with the New York Philharmonic as part of the American commitment to the Osaka World's Fair. I was reluctant to go on this trip because of various unpleasant memories of World War II, but I swallowed my feelings in favor of a new adventure with the peripatetic maestro.

Not surprisingly we started with concerts in Osaka itself—concerts that might never have taken place if it hadn't been for a resurgence of my wartime aviation skills! Our 707 charter pilot and his crew literally could not find the Osaka airport through the brown haze of pollution blanketing the city and its environs. As a former

China-Burma-India troop carrier pilot I'd been invited to
the cockpit for our landing, and while everyone searched
around for the airport I followed suit. It happened I was
the first to spot it, quite far off to our left. I tapped the
pilot's shoulder and pointed. He took a few moments to
get his bearings and finally saw it as well, making a course
correction while calling out to the crew that all was now
okay. He turned and thanked me. I told him he was
welcome.

On arrival we were surrounded by an enormous
array of cheery people, all obviously delighted to have us
in their midst. The looks on those faces were quite different from the ones I'd seen in wartime Burma and China.
I glanced around for a few moments, taking in the excitement and pleasure, the posters and pictures and welcoming banners and voices calling "Renny!" and finally
decided to push back the past into the lower recesses of
memory and start anew.

Our daily activities included not only concerts but
also frequent visits to Kabuki, No theater, temples, gardens, receptions, and meetings with Japanese artists.
Lenny had a letter of introduction to one of these, the
writer Yukio Mishima, whose novels were causing quite a
stir in the West. From Osaka the two men talked on the
phone and agreed to meet in Tokyo. Since I'd just read
his *Temple of the Golden Pavilion* and *The Sailor Who
Fell with Grace from the Sea* I was anxious to meet him
as well.

Lenny suggested I come for a few minutes after Mishima's arrival and leave after an appropriate, short social visit. He was anxious to discover for himself whether there might be sparks between the two of them that could conceivably lead to a collaboration of some kind.

The day and time arrived for their meeting. After a firm knocking on the suite door, I opened it, and there, seated on a sofa, was Mishima, dressed like a Roman gladiator — leather straps criss-crossing his entire body, tight short pants studded with metal buttons, and thick sandals laced around his ankles. His eyes were hypnotic, his voice sonorous and deep. He gripped my hand with strong muscles. As we sat down I noticed his pants hugged his body, leaving nothing to the imagination, and making, I thought, bodily movement extremely treacherous. I told him how much I enjoyed the two books I'd read and he seemed pleased. All three of us had a drink, and after ten minutes or so I arose to leave.

"So soon?" he said. "We've hardly begun to talk."

"I'm afraid so," I replied, looking properly disappointed. "I've some business matters to attend to. I'll leave you and the maestro in peace."

The next day Bernstein was strangely silent about their visit, telling me only that Mishima wanted him to see a film, to which I was also invited, and that someone was coming to pick us up at three o'clock that afternoon. "Someone" turned out to be three young men, all with

116

shaved heads and dressed in white uniforms with swords at their sides. They were members of Mishima's private army, an ultraconservative group of young people who stirred considerable public and private controversy by espousing the divinity of the emperor, the old warrior civilization, and the code of the samurai.

We were escorted across the street to the side door of a movie theater and asked to walk up some small, steep steps. Mishima was waiting for us on the top landing, dressed in a uniform similar to that of his troops.

"I made this film some time ago," he said, bowing in our direction. "I think it's one of my best."

We entered the screening room and took seats. The lights were lowered and what came on was the true story of a 1936 scandal involving a young warrior in the Imperial Household, a scandal that ended when the young man committed hara-kiri. The young man was played by Mishima himself, who also wrote the screenplay and directed the film. The hara-kiri was dragged to revolting lengths, all accompanied by a recorded soundtrack highlighting portions of *Tristan und Isolde*. I slipped lower and lower into my seat as the gore became worse; Lenny, uncharacteristically, sat bolt upright, watching the film but not making a sound. Usually in a theater or at a screening he squirmed around and wasn't shy at all about passing his opinions in stage whispers that could be heard in every corner of any auditorium. But not this time.

When the film was finally over, Lenny and I walked

back from our seats toward the projection booth to find Mishima, arms akimbo and jaw set, standing against the wall, staring at us.

"Well," he said, "what do you think?"

There was silence. Lenny just looked at him. I murmured something about the soundtrack.

"It seemed to give added dimension to what you were doing," I said, trying to break the silence.

"Of course!" he barked, as if I was some kind of class idiot. He kept his eyes on Lenny.

"And what do *you* think, Maestro?"

Lenny made no response, just stared back at him. Finally he said: "I need time to think."

We started out of the room and down the little stairs. I made a stab at saying good-bye but Mishima was only interested in Bernstein.

As our escorts reformed a little ring around us, Lenny looked back. Mishima saluted. We were then marched to our hotel.

On reaching his suite Lenny excused himself and bolted for the bathroom. I heard sounds of retching, then the toilet flushing and faucets running. He emerged shakily and poured himself a stiff drink. "My God, my God, how *unbearable*! No more of this, no more."

He and I were both deeply upset by the film and by Mishima himself, yet at the same time curious about this strange, dark, obsessed man who had a major talent for writing compelling prose.

Alas, we never found out any more about him. Two weeks after our meeting, Mishima, in a final burst of his puzzling personality, committed hara-kiri himself in front of all his young troops, whom he had called together for a rousing speech and martial demonstration of blood-and-fire traditions. As I write about him now, some twenty-two years after the fact, I wonder if his name and work will continue to remain an important part of the postwar culture of Japan.

Several breakfast meetings at the coffee shop in Tokyo's Imperial Hotel helped bring 1970 to a happy conclusion. Those meetings were the climax of weeks of on-again, off-again talks with Hans Andresen, a representative of Unitel, the Munich-based German television and film conglomerate eager for the maestro to film the four symphonies of Brahms and the nine of Gustav Mahler. Andresen had been dispatched by Leo Kirch, owner of the firm, to trail me from the Beethoven Birthday days in Vienna to London and New York and now to Tokyo. It seemed to me that the greater distance he traveled, the more zealous he became.

Lenny and I had thoroughly discussed his basic proposal, recognizing that it might be the windfall we were seeking to finance Amberson Productions. I asked Abe Freidman to find out about Kirch, who, it turned out, was making a fortune selling American television programs in Germany, and also had a passion for producing musical films. It appeared he believed in the future of such films

119

for European and Asian television as well as the then non-existent videocassette market. As a result, he had a number of serious artists under contract to his company, including Herbert von Karajan. Kirch wanted Lenny in order to have the world's two most glamorous conductors under his personal film-production wing.

Andresen and I finally reached an agreement in principle one morning over a couple of coffee shop boiled eggs. Although formal contracts had yet to be drawn up, and Lenny was with the Vienna Philharmonic on a European tour, we decided to press ahead with plans to film Mahler's Ninth Symphony in Berlin. The date was set for March 1971.

Several weeks after reaching this tentative understanding, final contracts were completed in New York. In addition to the Brahms and Mahler, Unitel would have exclusive rights to any television projects we might initiate. In return, they agreed to put up all production monies and to pay advances and fees to Amberson, an arrangement that suited us just fine.

When all points had been settled, and contract documents prepared under Friedman's redoubtable eyes, I took them to Lenny for signature. I sat with him in his study while he leafed through the pages in a desultory manner, asking few questions. Finally he came to the last page and I handed him my pen.

"Am I really going to sign a contract with a German company?" he murmured quietly. "I know I work in

Austria and Germany, but do I really want a long-term commitment there as well? It's hard, I just don't know."

That question was, in a very real sense, a philosophical one concerning Jew and German in the postwar world, but it was also the key to our production future. No American company had the slightest interest in our activities, with the single exception of the late Joseph Levine, whose Embassy Pictures, having been outrageously successful with spaghetti westerns and Mike Nichols's *The Graduate*, hoped to acquire Amberson essentially for the rights to Lenny's music. We went through an avalanche of relentless lawyers and countless awful meetings but finally ended up beating back Levine's proposals and continuing on our own. Unitel offered us the unique opportunity to have exactly what we desired: financing from the outside and creative control completely in our own hands.

"The war is over, Lenny," I said in equally quiet tones. "This contract is written by your own lawyer with every safeguard we can collectively think of. I feel you should sign it."

He looked up at me, biting his lower lip. It was a look I'd come to know well, midway between "should" and "won't." Finally he took a deep breath.

"OK. Let's see how it goes." He signed, underlining his signature. Amberson Productions now had a large part of its capital structure in place.

The contracts were signed in the fall of 1970. After a brief Christmas break, we went off to Paris in early 1971 for a special series of concerts with L'Orchestre de Paris.

Now, conducting French orchestras is always a tricky business. Players turn up for rehearsals but often send substitutes for the actual concerts. This has to do in part with antiquated work rules and in part with French quirkiness about artistic independence. Lenny knew about these caprices from earlier engagements, and his contract stipulated that the players who rehearsed were to be the players who performed. As a consequence of this proviso, when he mounted the podium for his first rehearsal, he looked out over a sullen group of musicians prepared to make his life unpleasant. I sat in the auditorium, waiting to pick up the pieces.

Lenny proceeded as if he'd just been given the warmest ovation of his life. In fluent French enhanced with appropriate Gallic gestures, he told the orchestra how pleased he was to be making music with them. On the program, divided between French and American repertoire, he'd planned to play and conduct the Piano Concerto in G Major of Ravel. I knew he hadn't practiced the piano for months, because he kept moaning and groaning and carrying on about canceling, but standing before the orchestra he spoke about the Concerto in glowing terms of love for this particularly sparkling tour de force of

French genius and, seating himself at the provided Bechstein, gave the downbeat.

He set a terrific tempo; the orchestra had to be on its collective toes to keep up. As a result of his body language, enthusiasm, and bravura, to say nothing of pianistic virtuosity, the sullenness began to lift and slowly to be replaced by something resembling pleasure. At the end of the Concerto the orchestra was applauding.

There were six concerts in this particular series, the last to be performed at the Great Hall of the University of Paris. The auditorium itself is inoffensively modern; filled, it looks rather like a large Wedgwood saucer. By the time of this concert, Lenny and the orchestra had become fast friends, mutually delighted to be surrounded by a house packed to the rafters with students. Those who couldn't find seats jammed themselves into the aisles and exits; their exuberance was contagious. By the end of the evening the applause and cheering almost hurt the ears. As a final gesture, and after countless curtain calls, Lenny threw his baton into the crowd and ran off stage. He was promptly caught and brought to a large open area near the stage and besieged by students eager to talk.

And there he remained, engaged in avid conversation with them, for more than two hours. His lifelong interest in young people knew no bounds; he would have gladly continued on all night. We were due, however, to leave Paris in two days for Vienna to begin rehearsals for a reprise of his 1968 production of *Der Rosenkavalier*, as well as for our first Unitel project. There was a lot of hard work ahead, and I didn't want an overexhausted maestro struggling against fatigue. So I rallied the university guards, who in rather splendid fashion and without a show of strength or force persuaded the students to return to their rooms, simultaneously turning out the auditorium lights.

Lenny was too elated by the evening to be in any mood for sleep. He rounded up a group of friends, and we all made our way over to Les Halles to sample onion soup and *oursins*, finally arriving back at our hotel around 6:00 A.M. I kept reminding him that we had to leave for Vienna the following day, but he paid no attention. I finally gave up, deciding to abandon the group to his agenda and let tomorrow take care of itself.

When that day arrived, there was a lot of hugging and many warm good-byes; indeed, there were so many farewells that we were late leaving the hotel. As a result we were caught at the wrong hour in Paris's hideous morning traffic and arrived at Orly Airport with only minutes to spare. We raced to the Vienna gate only to be told by a smug Air France employee that the flight was closed. I looked out and saw the plane still on the ground.

"We must get on that plane!" I said to the gate-keeper. "There's a large group of people meeting Maestro Bernstein in Vienna, and he has opera rehearsals this afternoon."

"The flight is closed, Monsieur," came the prim reply. "Fermé, fermé, fermé."

"But there must be someone who can help us," I pleaded.

Lenny looked over at me. "You stay here and see what you can do. I'll try to find a manager." He took off, running down the corridor, coattails flapping.

In a couple of minutes he was back with an official who clapped his hands—the gates were opened and a covered jeep brought to the door. The official herded us into the vehicle, piling in our considerable hand luggage. From out of nowhere two attractive stewardessess appeared and got in as well. We lurched away from the gate down the tarmac, coming to a halt about 50 yards from the open rear door of our plane. I noticed soldiers standing about, submachine guns slung over their shoulders.

"We have a hijack alert," the official said. "That's why all the security. You two get out of the jeep behind the stewardesses. They will distract the soldiers. Run for that ramp door. But hurry!"

We ducked and ran, starting up the ramp just as it began folding into the plane. We were literally hurtled into the cabin, our hand luggage flying every which way. As we stood up it was impossible not to notice the rear-seated passengers looking at us with irritated disdain. We mustered whatever dignity we could manage and walked slowly forward to our first-class seats. As we sat down, exhausted from all the fuss, Lenny glanced out his window. There were the stewardessess, our official, and the soldiers, all saluting. We saluted and waved back.

Arrival in Vienna meant immediately getting to work on *Der Rosenkavalier* and production planning for the Mahler Ninth, but not before the Opern Ball.

The Opern Ball, the high point of Vienna's social season, is held in the State Opera House, which closes for two days before the event to take out all the orchestra seats and wax the floor for dancing. White tie is required, decorations strongly encouraged. Lenny and I were invited to be the guests of the Israeli ambassador in his box. I ran around Vienna trying to rent tails—I wasn't the only one, however, and was unable to find any. At the last minute, Herbert Kloiber, Karajan's godson and sales manager for Unitel, lent me his. They were elegant and fit surprisingly well. The only problem was that they were tailored out of a thick, durable material that could almost stand in the corner by itself.

Since neither Felicia nor Betty was along on the first part of this trip, Lenny and I invited Lily Schoenburg to be our joint date, and the three of us swept into the opera house together. From the ambassador's box we looked down on the swirling dancers: it was a nineteenth-century engraving come to life. Lily and I danced, and with each step my borrowed clothes tightened like a vise, squeezing in the heat. We waltzed constantly in the same direction—I was told any other way is not Viennese—and I

126

concentrated on not becoming seasick. Lily remained cool and collected throughout. I retained my composure; it took some doing, but it was a classic case of mind over matter.

Lenny got on the floor and people made way for him. He danced conservatively and bowed a lot. The women, on the whole, were rather dowdy; the men, in their tails and decorations, looked much grander. Here and there one could spot a Parisian dress, or someone wearing clothes with a touch of style, but on the whole this was not easy to find.

The maestro soon became bored with the whole affair and took his leave. Lily and I stayed until the wee hours, returning to her home in a horse-drawn carriage. It was a romantic evening from start to finish.

We were now able to proceed with our preparations for both the State Opera performances and a CBS recording of *Der Rosenkavalier* with Lenny's handpicked cast. Christa Ludwig, Gwyneth Jones, Walter Berry, Lucia Popp, and Placido Domingo were all Bernstein's friends as well as his colleagues. Rehearsals, except for the first one, were always exciting, as various ideas came together. The first, however, almost lost him the entire project.

What happened was this: He called the soloists for a piano rehearsal the afternoon we arrived from Paris, to begin at 5:00 P.M. in the great hall of the Sofiensäle, where Johann Strauss used to lead his orchestra, and where the CBS recording was to be made. When they arrived, he cheerfully announced that they were going to go through the entire opera together without stopping. Of course, they stopped frequently for his comments, but never for a rest-break. I watched as they all grew more and more annoyed.

Finally, at around 10:00 P.M., Walter Berry approached me; he made it clear that for the first time in his life Lenny was about to find himself on the receiving end of a mutiny. "We all know this piece backwards and forwards, even if he doesn't remember it," he hissed in my ear. "Tell him to stop already. Enough is enough." I looked up to see Christa nodding in my direction, as well as Gwyneth, Lucia, and even Placido. Lenny was totally oblivious to the imminent insurrection; he was busy conducting with a pencil, completely caught up in the music.

I hastily scribbled a note of warning and slipped it onto his score. "What?" he yelled when he saw it, "Stop? Impossible!"

"Oh yes, Maestro," came Berry's rolling tones. "We're dying here." With that he sank to his knees, clutching his throat, and slowly collapsed on the floor. Within seconds Christa, Gwyneth, and Lucia did the same thing. Catching the mood, the peerless Opera House pianist finished whatever phrase he was playing and stopped with his hands frozen on the keys.

Lenny looked at them all and then over at me. I held up five fingers, pointing to a nearby clock. He shook his

head no. I nodded yes. The singers were now all lying
down. I knew that battle lines were being drawn. Finally
I saw a smile start across his mouth.

"One hour for dinner?" I called out.

"No," Lenny answered, "two if you'll all agree to
come back and finish the opera. And this time we'll go
straight to the end without stopping. I promise!" Then he
started around the room hugging and kissing everyone,
ending up with the pianist. While this was going on I
alerted the Sofiensäle canteen staff, who brought in piles
of sandwiches, wine, beer, and coffee.

Everyone pounced on the food and drink, which
quickly acted as a restorative. Around midnight the
rehearsal resumed. True to his word, Lenny went right to
the end without comment except for his occasional enthusiastic reactions when particular moments touched him.
Gradually he brought the singers back into his fold; by the
end everyone was exhausted but excited.

A few days later, with rehearsals moving along
smoothly, I took the opportunity to arrange an audition
for a young American dramatic soprano who was willy-
nilly determined to sing for the maestro. She was a client
of my friend Harry Beall, one of the better New York concert managers, who had written me about her. When I
received the letter I quickly called Harry to say there was
not time for such business but was too late; the young lady
had already arrived in Vienna and made it plain that she
had no intention of leaving until she was heard.

Since she was a fellow American, and Harry Beall a friend, I suggested we might as well get it over with and booked the Opera House chorus room one morning before regular *Der Rosenkavalier* rehearsals.

"Why?" asked the maestro. "I've no operatic plans beyond what we're doing here."

"Humor me, then," I replied. "Let's hear her."

At the appointed time, into the chorus room walked a large, intimidating woman, regal and assured, followed by a short man who was obviously her accompanist. As she advanced toward the piano it was impossible to get any sense of her other than her towering size and fiercely handsome face. Lenny and I looked at each other in disbelief, but before we could say anything she announced that she would start with Elisabeth's great aria "Dich teure Halle" from *Tannhäuser.* Her voice rang out with such power and musicality that we were stunned. When she came to the last line, "Du teure Halle, sei mir gegrüsst," the walls vibrated with her conviction. Before we could make any comments, she announced that she would continue with the "Liebestod" from *Tristan und Isolde.* "Mild und leise wie er lächelt" floated into the room, sure, compelling, and deeply moving. Finishing, she barely took a breath before launching into the *Götterdämmerung* Immolation Scene. At the end, as the ringing tones of the stirring last lines "Siegfried! Siegfried! Sieh! Selig grüsst dich dein Weib!" died away, we sat in absolute silence.

Appearing to be no more exhausted than if she'd just sung a few nursery rhymes, our queenly visitor picked up her music, thanked the pianist, who looked as bewildered as we felt, and started toward the door. Lenny ran after her. "Wait, wait," he called, "sit a moment and let's talk."

"Thank you, Maestro," she replied, "but I've a train to catch. I just wanted you to hear me. Someday I hope we work together." She put out her hand to say good-bye.

After she left, Lenny asked: "Who was that *incredible* woman?"

I couldn't remember her name and, scrounging through my pockets to find some notes, finally pulled out Harry's letter. "Her name is Jessye Norman," I read aloud. Lenny and I looked at each other, stupefied for a moment. We would never forget that incident, nor that voice.

While *Der Rosenkavalier* performances proceeded apace, rehearsals began for the Mahler Ninth. Humphrey Burton joined us to film those rehearsals as a separate documentary on the process itself, culminating in the final run-through on a February afternoon in the Musikverein. The cameras were able to catch the communication between conductor and players, especially as the orchestra was becoming immersed in the music and beginning to understand Bernstein's particular intensity about Gustav Mahler.

To understand this intensity, it's necessary to know that the Ninth Symphony reflects the conflicts that haunted the composer his whole life. Mahler was a sensitive artist who knew he had little time to live, who was, in fact, killing himself. His entire creative life was about conflict. As Bernstein himself put it, Mahler never ceased to struggle against himself. It was "Mahler the creator versus Mahler the performer; the Jew versus the Christian; the Believer versus the Doubter; the Naif versus the Sophisticate; the provincial Bohemian versus the Viennese 'homme du monde'; the Faustian philosopher versus the Oriental mystic; the Operatic Symphonist who never wrote an opera — but mainly the battle raged between Western man at the turn of the century and the life of the spirit."

It is curious that, in one way or another, all of these points (except, of course, for the one about opera, since Lenny wrote two operas as well as the operetta *Candide*) applied to Bernstein himself, a man forever trapped between the political and scientific horrors of our age and the potential strength and beauty in mankind. These inner ragings of his found their best and fullest moments of artistic expression when he was performing the Mahler symphonies, although they drained him physically and mentally. This was especially true of the Ninth, a summing up of Mahlerian thought and an embrace of death. I was always very glad to see him step down from the

132

podium still in one piece after conducting that particular work.

It took a while for the Vienna Philharmonic to cotton to the strange kinship between Mahler and Bernstein, but when they finally did the results were gripping. Under Bernstein's baton, they were playing these symphonies for almost the first time since the end of World War II. When Hitler was in power, of course, Mahler's music was banned; and though there was still a sprinkling of older musicians in the orchestra who remembered Bruno Walter's performances before the 1938 *Anschluss*, most of the personnel were younger and had never heard any of Mahler's music at all, let alone played it. We wanted to capture on film as much of this sense of discovery as possible, because it really was a three-way adventure between composer, orchestra, and conductor.

Although these Vienna days and nights were filled with rehearsals, performances, and recordings, there was also time for the occasional break. One of these was earmarked for what looked to be a particularly pleasant occasion.

The Austrian town of Bernstein, nestled in the Burgenland mountains some 50 miles south of Vienna and close to the Hungarian border, had decided to honor the maestro by renaming its municipal park Leonard Bernstein Platz. There'd been a great deal of planning for this project and a lot of publicity in the press. Felicia, who

133

really wasn't charmed by the Viennese, had flown over for the ceremonies with Phyllis Newman and her husband, Adolph Green. My wife, Betty, came as well. She and I took the opportunity to get away for a long weekend in the Semmering prior to the event.

On the appointed day we drove to Bernstein through some very pretty country, arriving before everyone else. The first thing we noticed was the absence of people. A few tattered banners were flapping in the breeze, but the streets were empty; the town looked deserted. We drove around, finally spotting a small tavern, where we went to ask about the ceremonies. When I identified myself the taverner grew quite agitated, telling me to sit while he made a telephone call. Presently we were joined by a very angry mayor, who shoved a telegram under my nose signed by Lenny, canceling his visit.

"We received this several hours ago. All the children were out in their best clothes, the band was ready to play. We sent everyone home!" He was plainly hurt as well as angry.

"But that's impossible," I replied. "The maestro will be here any moment. This wire is some kind of sick joke."

I looked out the window just as the car with Lenny, Felicia, and the Greens came into sight. I ran out onto the tavern's terrace and waved them over.

"Where is everybody?" Felicia asked. "We've been driving around and haven't seen a soul."

"I'm afraid we're all victims of some Viennese Bös-artig," I said, and I told them about the telegram.

'You're kidding,'' Lenny exclaimed, getting out of the car and following me into the tavern. I introduced him to the mayor, who was by now thoroughly confused.

"But you sent a telegram, Maestro," he said, handing it to him.

"I did no such thing," Lenny answered. "Someone in Vienna obviously wants to embarrass us both. This is terrible. What can we do to help?"

"Well," said the mayor, "there was to have been lunch after the ceremonies at the castle over there." He pointed to a huge building halfway up a mountain road. "That's our city hall; in the old days our local princes lived there. The food's probably still in the kitchen."

I asked about the children and the band, and whether some of them might be able to assemble at the castle. Lenny and Felicia were enthusiastic.

"We could have a wonderful time meeting them all and sharing whatever is around for lunch!" she said. "Come on, we'll make a party out of this awful business."

The mayor looked skeptical but obviously saw that we were all extremely upset, especially Lenny.

"I want to do *anything* I can do to help," he said.

The mayor went to the phone: the tavern owner ran out the back door to find the band leader; and we were soon joined by several others who were instructed to lead us to the castle. We got into our two cars and followed.

135

It wasn't long before other cars began to arrive, many discharging children still dressed in their best clothes, their floral headdresses only slightly faded. Felicia, Betty, and Phyllis formed a welcoming committee; Lenny immediately sat down and began talking to them in German. Presently we heard the sounds of the band, wending its way up the hill. The castle staff began bringing out trays of food, townspeople appeared, and before long the place was filled with confused but happy people.

When the mayor arrived, we all moved into the castle's main hall, where the band, now fully assembled, began to serenade us. Lenny went to the bandstand, as did Adolph Green, who was delighted to discover that many of the musicians spoke his family's native Hungarian. Both joined in the music making.

In short order the food appeared, and we all ate delicious cold cuts, washing it all down with excellent local beer. At the appropriate moment the mayor called for order and proceeded to make the speech he'd planned to deliver at the original ceremony. When his remarks were finished, the applause was loud and prolonged as everyone surrounded the maestro with obvious affection.

Piling back into our two cars, we headed for the municipal park. The crowds followed, and with much good cheer the new sign designating the area Leonard Bernstein Platz was duly unveiled. A final bow and waves from the maestro concluded the proceedings. By the time we started back to Vienna, we left behind a happy town, but we weren't going to rest until we'd found out who'd sent the telegram.

Unfortunately, we never discovered the identity of the perpetrator, although various people were convinced that he or she was some friend of Herbert von Karajan. All we were able to find out was the post-office branch from which the telegram had been sent; the branch was directly opposite the front door of the Volksoper. However, no employee remembered anything about its transmission. To this day the mystery remains unsolved.

A couple of days after this incident—Felicia, Betty, Phyllis, and Adolph were by now back in America—Lenny's Vienna Philharmonic European tour began in Munich. I flew ahead to Berlin to work on Mahler production details.

As with the Verdi Requiem, we decided to gamble: one of the three public performances was canceled and replaced by a day of filming before an invited audience. Musically this was a splendid idea, as the piece was being played every other night on the tour. Logistically, however, it posed a number of problems.

First of all we were working with 35 millimeter film instead of the customary videotape. This meant bringing tons of equipment—including heavy cameras, batteries of lights and generators, crates of film, massive stereo sound console systems—and a host of personnel—grips, gaffers, assistant directors, timekeepers, and wardrobe people—into the Philharmonie, West Berlin's concert hall, which was new at that time but already showing signs of wear and tear and crumbling masonry. The Philharmonie is normally the home of the Berlin Philharmonic. From a design standpoint, it is one of the few successful new concert halls, the performers surrounded by the audience without in any sense being intermingled with them. It's like a huge living room with lots of entrances and exits. Intimacy is achieved without shoulder rubbing, creating a warm atmosphere for players and audience alike. Unhappily, it also poses an array of difficulties for photography and lighting. Many of these had been carefully defined beforehand by Humphrey, who was to direct, and by Fritz Buttenstedt, Unitel's production overlord. The three of us met in Berlin a week before the filming to iron out whatever last-minute details remained and to deal with problems between our production requirements and the management of both the Philharmonie and the Berlin Philharmonic.

Curiously, there was only one real issue. Karajan, the conductor of the Berlin Philharmonic, who also had a contract with Unitel, insisted on dubbing his films: that is, having the orchestra record the sound track before the photography and then playing back the sound while the cameras rolled. Lenny wanted to avoid this technique at all costs, feeling that the results were stilted, looked fake, and conveyed none of the concentration and emotional impact of a live performance. Unitel was stubbornly wedded to the Karajan technique and extremely skeptical about our approach. I had to do a lot of talking to get our points across, finally resorting to putting the situation on an either/or basis. I knew that the Berlin Philharmonic management would be watching our method carefully as a consequence of the often unspoken but very real competition between the two conductors. It came down to the fact that we were trying a new technique in Karajan's home territory; I wanted to avoid stepping on toes, but we were going to do it our way.

On 10 March 1971 we began our one-day shoot, and from the beginning were blasted with problems. The schedule called for camera rehearsals from 11:00 A.M. to 1:00 P.M., followed by two filming sessions with audience, from 5:00 P.M. to 7:00 P.M. and from 8:00 P.M. to 10:00 P.M. Twenty minutes before the cameras were to roll, the young assistant director, an expert on Unitel film techniques, had a heart seizure. He insisted that he wanted to carry out his responsibilities, but the doctors forbade him to do so. Since he was the only one who fully understood the mysteries of film magazines, he left Humphrey in the awkward spot of having to ad-lib instead of having someone at his elbow who could warn him when each camera's film was running out. Since we wanted no interruptions in the shooting, every camera had its own film boy crouched alongside, ready to replace magazines as needed. The assistant director was the straw boss of this group; the boys now had to learn a new system under pressure. In addition, the sound equipment had unexpected difficulties with stereo spread and miking; a third of the big arc lamps kept blowing out; and the temperature in the hall was arctic. Outside a blizzard raged and if all that wasn't enough, Bernstein had intestinal flu. As our carefully laid plans crumbled, I wondered what on earth I was doing here, stuck in the middle of what looked like certain disaster.

But as is often the case, talented heads prevailed. When 5:00 P.M. rolled around we were prepared—tense and on edge to be sure, but that's not a bad mood for the Mahler Ninth. The performance was musically compelling. I looked out at the audience and saw the attention they were giving to what they were hearing. I spent some of the performance in the sound booth helping in any way I could, but mostly I stayed out of the way while the experts did their jobs. By 11:30 P.M. they had done it well; an exhausted but exhilarated Bernstein was ready for supper at the home of the American minister to Berlin, Brewster Morris.

We drove to the Morrises in the teeth of a winter storm that had been howling and swirling all day, arriving after midnight. I'd warned our host and hostess that we'd be late and they hadn't seemed to mind. We were welcomed with open arms and greeted by the cream of Berlin artistic and cultural life. Lenny was pleased to see everyone, but it was obvious that he was still battling flu.

The next day we flew to Hamburg. Lenny was still feeling rotten and by the middle of the day had begun to run a high fever. He went to bed the minute we arrived at the Vier Jahreszeiten Hotel, and I sent for a doctor. The physician, after careful examination of his eminent patient, decreed exhaustion, the grippe, and intestinal upset. He ordered us to cancel the concert, which Lenny clearly had no intention of doing. The doctor bowed, clicked his heels, and stated that he would accept no further responsibility for the consequences. He then presented me with his bill. That night the maestro was literally carried to the concert hall, but the minute he put his foot on the stage his illness seemed to disappear. It returned with a vengeance when the concert was over, however. We carried him home and put him to bed. Lenny looked more dead than alive and for the first time he alarmed me. I decided to spend the night on the sofa in the living room of his suite, just in case something happened. At about 5:00 A.M. he awoke, hungry. I could hear him ordering food from room service.

"Order some for me, too," I croaked from the couch. "Breakfast!"

When it arrived we both ate with gusto. There was no trace of illness; the miraculous Bernstein constitution had snapped back into place.

Shortly after the Hamburg concert we sat down to complete plans for 1971's biggest adventure, the opening of the John F. Kennedy Center for the Performing Arts in Washington, D.C.

Some three years earlier, Lenny had accepted an

141

invitation from Jacqueline Kennedy Onassis and the Center's chairman, his old friend Roger L. Stevens, to compose the inaugural work. At various times we talked about what kind of piece he might do, and almost from the first he began developing an idea to honor the Kennedy memory with a contemporary variation of the Mass. He'd always been fascinated by Catholic ritual and long knew that he wanted to do something theatrical with the traditional Mass, perhaps modernizing it and bringing it to bear on present-day political, social, and spiritual problems; this seemed the perfect occasion for such a project. At this point, however, he was beginning to panic. The piece was nowhere near finished and it was already mid-March. Less than six months remained before the Center's opening, scheduled for 8 September 1971; there was no chance of postponement. Since he had to finish the Vienna Philharmonic tour and put the final touches on the *Der Rosenkavalier* recording before he could concentrate on composing, I could see the oh-my-God-what-am-I-going-to-do look beginning to settle on his face.

Two things had to be done immediately: he needed a collaborator-lyricist to help with the text, particularly those parts that were not drawn directly from the liturgy of the Mass, and a director who might be able to take what he'd already done and begin making theatrical sense of it. To fill the latter position, Roger Stevens, Robby Lantz, and I held a series of trans-Atlantic phone calls. We drew up lists of possibilities, concurring that the director would obviously have to be someone whose creative bent meshed with Lenny's and who would be relentless in pushing him to complete the task.

It wasn't easy to work all of this out long-distance, but we had little choice until the tour and recording sessions were completed. When we returned home at the end of April, Lenny made the final decision to invite Gordon Davidson to take on the directorial responsibilities. Gordon and Lenny knew each other from various concert collaborations, and after positive preliminary discussion happily agreed to work together.

It remained to find a collaborator-lyricist. On the recommendations of several friends, and especially his sister, Shirley, a theatrical agent, Lenny went to see *Godspell* and was impressed by the lyrics of her client, the young Stephen Schwartz. Schwartz himself was somewhat caught up in his own success and rather imperious about defining his views of collaboration. Lenny, however, overlooked this personal grandness and offered him the job. Schwartz accepted.

With these positions filled, the production could now move into high gear. Alvin Ailey was tapped for the choreography and brought his company into the cast. Auditions were held for the leading roles; we were particularly concerned to find just the right person to play the Celebrant of the Mass—he had to be young, intense,

143

compelling, and able to sing as well as act. Various people presented themselves but none seemed to have all the qualities we were seeking.

Then, on a hot, early June afternoon, a young man walked into our barren rehearsal hall and began singing in a rich baritone, accompanying himself on the guitar. His sound made us all look up: his strength and ability to communicate were startling. When he finished Lenny asked him to talk with us. Within minutes we knew we'd found our Celebrant. A member of the New York City Opera, he had, prior to embarking on a singing career, worked in a mental hospital and while there married a fellow staff member. Both he and his wife were touched and tortured by the problems of the mentally ill and determined to alleviate suffering wherever they could. Still a young man, he'd lived an unusual, people-oriented life, and his experiences showed in his work. His name was Alan Titus. I had a feeling that his name would become well known if the Mass project succeeded.

During May and June Bernstein and Schwartz kept turning out material, which Gordon and Alvin worked into shape for the stage; Oliver Smith began to design the sets, and Gilbert Helmsley, Jr., the lighting. Herman Shumlin's wife, Diana, took on the tough task of coordinating the whole production, made particularly difficult by the fact that we had no formal production budget. Roger Stevens was busy handling the myriad Kennedy Center problems and couldn't spend any time overseeing our show.

He and I agreed that I would become the associate producer and meet with him a couple of times a week to go over issues.

We were making progress on all fronts until word reached us one afternnon that Roger had suffered a sudden heart attack. Lenny, who hated anything to do with illnesses or hospitals, was beside himself with worry. Roger was not only leading the public and private battles to establish the Kennedy Center, he had been the key producer and investor in the original *West Side Story*, as well as the first to recognize what we were trying to do with Amberson Productions. Now we were told that he might not pull through, and in great shock Lenny rushed to the hospital to be at his side.

He was greeted there by grim-faced doctors and told to wait. Finally, after several hours, he was taken to Roger's room, where a pale figure in a web of tubes and wires lay quietly awake.

As Lenny told me, and Roger later confirmed, he approached the bed as if prepared to view a dead body, his eyes wide, voice tremulous, and hands shaking. Looking down at Roger, Lenny's eyes were warm with compassion, and he asked if there was *anything* he could do to help. (Memories of a town in Austria!)

"Yes, there is," Roger replied softly, beckoning him to lean closer. "There's one thing I need badly."

"What's that?" asked Lenny in a frightened low whisper. "Tell me what to do."

"Finish *Mass*," he said, in a stage whisper that could be heard by the hovering doctors and nurses. "I'll be out of here soon and don't want to come back. Finish my piece!"

Lenny always said the hospital visit scared him sufficiently that he wrote around-the-clock until *Mass* was finished. It was just as well, because in early August we moved everyone to the almost-finished Kennedy Center and began our final preparations in the Opera House.

At that point we engaged Maurice Peress as music director and conductor for what was now called *Mass, A Theatre Piece for Singers, Players and Dancers*. Peress, a former assistant conductor of the New York Philharmonic during the Bernstein years, was eager and knowledgeable and fit in easily with the rest of the creative group. I felt for him, though, at one particular rehearsal.

Mass has two orchestral "Meditations," interludes just before the Gloria and the Epistle. They are beautiful, but complex and difficult to play. Peress was rehearsing the first one, but Lenny was visibly unhappy with the tempo and sound. At one point he walked down to the orchestra pit and, leaping over the railing, picked up Peress's baton. In a couple of minutes he had that group of local Washington players sounding as if they were the Vienna Philharmonic. I was with Alvin Ailey in the middle of the theater at the time and we both sat bolt upright at the astounding sound. "Yeah, man," said Alvin quietly, "that's what it's all about!"

When he was finished, Lenny turned around and spoke to Peress. "See, Maurice?" he said. "OK?" And he gave him a big hug.

In a few days everything was ready for a rough run-through, at which, as the performance got underway, we all began to feel that a very exciting theatrical event was being created. It was, however, too long, and I asked Gordon Davidson to dinner to share my feelings. He indicated that he agreed completely, but said that Lenny was touchy on the subject and not interested in discussing it.

"You and Roger will have to help," he said. "I'll do all I can, and so will Alvin and everyone else. But you and Roger must keep after him." I promised we would.

We did, but to no avail. Lenny simply would not hear a word about cuts and the closer we got to the opening, the more stubborn he became. We tried talking to him individually and collectively, but all we got for our pains were hurt silences.

We got a lot of howls, though, from his collaborator. When the first copies of the house programs were delivered, Schwartz sought out Diana and myself, marching into the Kennedy Center restaurant where we were lunching to scream that he would close the show unless his credits were improved. He threatened injunctions, pickets, and every manner of disturbance, as the other restaurant patrons listened in horrified fascination. His complaint was not completely unjustified—there had been a mistake that needed quick repair—but his behavior was unnecessary. When he had finished his tirade and left, the other patrons expressed their sympathy for us. We thanked them.

Schwartz cooled down just before the public dress rehearsal, after which Roger, Gordon, and I again approached Lenny about cuts. By this time he was exhausted, and finally, at some ungodly hour in the morning, he agreed to try Gordon's specific suggestions for the one formal preview we were doing just before opening night. However, Bernstein made us all promise that if he didn't like them they'd be eliminated and the original restored for the opening. We agreed to his terms, but in my heart I was counting on Felicia's help. She was coming down from New York for the preview and had not seen any of the work during rehearsals. She was the one person whose theatrical judgment Lenny trusted.

That particular night the work really took off. Everything fell into place, and at its conclusion the audience wouldn't leave. Proof of its power was borne out for me when I ran into William Safire, then President Nixon's chief speech writer, and his wife as the audience finally began trickling out. Safire must have known that Lenny was on Nixon's enemies list, but nonetheless grabbed my arm, and in a shaky, emotional voice said, "The chief's got to see this!"

We were all deeply moved, no one more so than Lenny himself, and we returned to the hotel elated. We should have known better. As soon as we walked into his suite he turned and said, "Tonight you've all had your fun. Everything goes back in tomorrow."

And that's what happened, despite Felicia's firm arguments on our behalf. Opening night arrived, and while the work was generally judged a success, it never was the triumph it might have been had the cuts and trimming been retained.

I've thought about this issue often, with regard not only to Bernstein but also to other creative friends, and I've come to the conclusion that as a general rule the creative person is frequently the worst judge of his or her own material. They often lose objectivity, forgetting they are creating something they want other people to share. That's why there will always be room for the impresario or producer, whose prime job it is to keep that objectivity to the fore.

The Kennedy Center opening marked a milestone in my relationship with the maestro. He knew I'd always harbored fantasies about running the Metropolitan Opera; both he and Felicia, to say nothing of my wife, were amused at this quirky, childhood idea. But in 1971, when the Met board picked our mutual friend Goeran Gentele to succeed Sir Rudolf Bing as general manager, they all, including Betty, urged me to accept Goeran's invitation to become his second in command. We agreed that Amberson business arrangements could be altered to accommodate my new position by bringing Harry Kraut on board to take my place and later setting up a series of business trusts with Harry and myself as trustees.

The changing of the guard took place a few days after the Kennedy Center festivities. Over a splendid dinner at the Bernstein country retreat in Connecticut, and with Lenny's benediction, I agreed to join Gentele at the Metropolitan on October 1, to begin nine months of joint on-the-job observation before he took over full responsibility.

Carmen and
Andromache

Goeran Gentele took over as the new general manager
of the Metropolitan Opera on 1 July 1972 and
shortly thereafter left for a brief holiday in
Sardinia. Gentele was not only the new
leader of one of the world's great opera companies but also a distinguished theater director in his own right. He had earlier made the decision to
open his first season by staging the new Barenreiter edition of *Carmen*. Lenny, who liked this bright, cheerful,
and talented Swede, agreed to conduct the opera, which
had a strong cast headed by Marilyn Horne, James
McCracken, Teresa Stratas, and Tom Krause. He was
also pleased to be reunited with Alvin Ailey, whom, at his

suggestion, Gentele engaged as the choreographer. The physical production itself, just then emerging from the Met's scenery shops, was designed to Gentele's specifications by the imaginative Czech, Josef Svoboda. I was responsible for seeing that everything about this project was ready by August 1, when rehearsals were set to begin.

Anticipation and excitement ran very high at the Met in those fresh new days, and similar feelings overtook the Bernstein household as well, where Lenny was studying a score he loved and Felicia and the children were delighted to have him home instead of dashing around the globe on guest engagements.

But this benign time wasn't to last for long. On July 18, Gentele and two of his children were killed as the rented car he was driving smashed head-on into a truck loaded with cement on a twisting, narrow Sardinian road. His wife, Marit, and a daughter by an earlier marriage survived. Suddenly, in a blinding flash, the responsibility for running the Metropolitan Opera fell to me. I felt as I always imagined Harry Truman must have felt in April 1945 when he heard the news that Franklin D. Roosevelt was dead.

Like Truman, I had little time for personal grief. I spent that first night on the telephone to people all over the world, but one of the most important calls I made was to the Bernsteins, who were staying in a rented house in the Berkshires while Lenny conducted and taught at Tanglewood. I broke the news to Felicia first, and when Lenny came to the phone I said I could not find any other way of telling him except straight out. After a few moments of shocked disbelief he caught his breath, saying we both now owed Goeran Gentele a brilliant *Carmen*.

At Lenny's suggestion I conferred with Jerome Robbins, who'd been a Gentele admirer, and asked him to take over the project. Jerry came to my office and we looked at the designs together. He asked for a day to think and finally declined on the grounds that his ideas would be restricted by the strong confines of the Svoboda sets. He wrote me a charming letter, however, saying it really didn't matter who directed the production, that in essence it was already a "world success" because of its conductor, cast, and sympathy for the Gentele tragedy.

A day after the Robbins visit, I again talked with the maestro. This time we discussed the real possibility of offering the task to Gentele's directorial assistant, a young man named Bodo Igesz who had been Franco Zeffirelli's assistant when Lenny made his Met debut conducting the 1964 production of *Falstaff*.

"What about him?" I asked. "He conferred with Gentele, he knows the piece, you like him, and I think the two of you could work well together."

"Let me think about it," came the reply. "It might be the right answer. I'll call you back."

I checked the Met's rehearsal department and learned that Igesz was at the Santa Fe Opera. I called and,

153

after the first expressions of sympathy, brought the conversation around to *Carmen.*

"How much work did the two of you do together before Gentele went off?" I asked.

"A little but not too much," came the reply. "We just got started. We were to develop details when he returned. You know he went off to think through the problems and complete his own planning. If there were any notebooks he took them with him."

"When do you finish up in Santa Fe?" I asked.

"At the end of the summer," he replied.

"I'll be in touch," I said.

Lenny called the next morning to say he'd been thinking things over and, realizing he had some strong ideas of his own about the production, would be happy to collaborate with Igesz. Could I please arrange for them to meet as soon as possible?

I put in another call to New Mexico and asked Igesz if he'd like the assignment. For a long moment there was silence on the line.

"Are you there?" I asked finally.

"Oh, yes," came the answer. "I'm just trying to think what I should do."

"It's a wonderful opportunity," I said, "your first real crack at the major leagues."

More silence. Finally, almost solemnly, Igesz agreed. He asked that I talk with John Crosby, the director of the Santa Fe Opera, to arrange an adjustment in his commitments and free him to fly back and forth between New Mexico and New York for the remaining summer weeks. Crosby was understanding and cooperative; the details were quickly ironed out.

On 1 August 1972 I took Lenny down to the orchestra rehearsal room and welcomed him back to the Metropolitan, where he'd last appeared three seasons earlier when he had conducted *Cavalleria Rusticana*. *Carmen* was his third Met production and, as it turned out, his last. Although he and Igesz had worked to sort out their basic directorial ideas during those hectic July weeks, they had not as yet discussed details with the anxious cast. Lenny was also not feeling well, plagued by an intestinal infection that seemed to resist treatment. He never said a word about his problem to me, however, knowing I now had my own hands full of unexpected responsibilities.

As it happened, the *Carmen* production developed a whole new host of problems on its own. Just as rehearsals were getting under way our Micaela, Teresa Stratas, canceled. We scurried around to find a proper replacement, finally settling on the almost unknown Adriana Maliponte. Michael Tilson Thomas, then at the beginning of his conducting career, was scheduled to take over the production following Bernstein's performances; he withdrew. I decided to hold off finding his replacement until we knew what kind of production we would actually achieve.

The Svoboda sets themselves were bulky and difficult to handle; but they were stark and dramatic, including thick rugs spread over various parts of the stage. This
meant potent and brilliant lighting plots that, for maximum effect, required more of the then existing Met elec-
trical facilities than they could deliver. Svoboda and the
Met's chief electrician were frequently at odds. The cast
was nervous about the French dialogue (the Barenreiter
edition returned the opera to its original form, with spoken lines rather than recitatives) and hated the idea of
what they perceived to be sound-swallowing rugs. The
rugs, necessary for special visuals, had been made of a
material that did not absorb sound. But Marilyn Horne
wouldn't believe our claim and was not shy about
expressing her views: either the rugs went or she did.
(Happily this problem soon became a nonproblem. At one
stage rehearsal, Lenny persuaded James McCracken to
lie down and let fly with an assortment of well-chosen
vocal phrases while he took Horne out into the auditorium
to hear for herself. She heard loud and clear.)

Just as that matter was settled, an uproar com-
menced over the removal of the prompter's box. The
prompter's box, a holdover from the nineteenth century,
had become a crutch on which many artists had grown to
depend for cues and entrances and indications of stage
business. It serves a role, to be sure, when an artist is a
last-minute replacement and doesn't know his or her way
around a particular set; but it is greatly overused by those

who know their roles well and simply lean on the prompter rather than rely on their own memories. Early on Gentele had decided to do away with the device for his *Carmen*; his cast would have to commit to memory all the music, dialogue, and stage business. The sets were designed without a place for the box. When Horne saw it was missing, she let her displeasure be known; once again she proffered an ultimatum: either the box would be there or she wasn't going to be. Other cast members supported her on this point, making it clear that with the many changes from a conventional *Carmen* they all needed to be certain no mistakes were made. I gave in. Svoboda wasn't happy about this decision because the resulting cuts in the carpets meant relighting, but he took it with good grace and the work was done.

While all these tensions abounded, the actual music and dramatic rehearsals were going remarkably well. Lenny and Igesz and Alvin Ailey were turning out to be a splendid team, but we all knew the true test would come with the audience at the dress rehearsal.

On Friday, September 11, we had our answer. The first public sign of a different *Carmen* came just before the statement of the "fate" theme in the overture: the house curtain slowly rose revealing a darkened Seville, one lone figure silhouetted in a shaft of light. Simultaneous with the overture's last harsh chord, full, bright hot sunlight hit the city. There was an audible gasp. When the lone silhouette figure of Don José walked slowly off into the crowd, the audience suddenly realized he was something more than Carmen's passionate, disappointed lover. It was, as critic and musicologist Harvey E. Phillips later wrote, "an indication not only that the tenor was intended to emerge as a more central character in the work—a protagonist whose downfall we would watch with as much interest as Carmen's own journey to death—but also the idea that fate, in all its mythic dimensions, would be the basis on which this production would succeed or fail."

Dress rehearsals at the Metropolitan are very much like performances. In theory a dress rehearsal can be stopped for corrections, and occasionally is, but for the most part this rarely happens. At the *Carmen* dress there was only one interruption. During the busy dialogue scene between Carmen and Don José that precedes her dance in Act II, McCracken, as Don José, while professing his overwhelming desire to make love, was unable to loosen his scabbard. In faultless American, Marilyn Horne interjected, "Sure, as soon as you take the sword off, *honey!*" The audience's laughter was an intense reaction of a group thoroughly captivated by what it was seeing and hearing. The house was with the artists. *Carmen* was working.

On September 19 the opening night performance surpassed all hopes. The critics went into raptures: "Daring and provocative," wrote the *New York Times*; "a triumph of continuity," said the *Post*; *New York* magazine

called Marilyn Horne's Carmen "one of the most remarkable minglings of endowments and intelligence I have wit-
nessed on any stage"; *Newsweek* commented that "as
Don José James McCracken gave one of his most spectacular performances"; and *Time* singled out Bernstein
for his "crackingly taut performance."

What New York saw that season was a *Carmen* without spit curls, a *Carmen*, as Harvey Phillips wrote, "that
rid itself of all the local trappings of operetta, all its pret-
tiness and with it the post-Bizet Guiraud recitatives. This
was a *Carmen* that went back to the original blood and
brutality of Mérimée, a *Carmen* that Gentele had seen as
a stylized tale of the collision between a man's barely sup-
pressed instinct for violence and the woman who cannot
resist it." It was quite a night.

There remained one more major hurdle: Lenny was
determined to record *Carmen*. The original contract I had
negotiated with Gentele contained this commitment; it
was up to me now, in my new role, to figure out a way to
honor it.

The Met itself had not been near a recording studio
since the early 1950s, when Columbia Records' devel-
opment of the LP led Goddard Lieberson to record a
memorable series of the standard repertoire. By 1972
American recording costs had risen to such an extent that
domestic opera recordings were no longer practical real-
ities. However, at this point Lenny was considering an
extraordinary offer from Deutsche Grammophon, a com-

pany anxious to gain something more than just a foothold in the American market.

Deutsche Grammophon's American artistic director, Thomas Mowrey, approached me with a proposal: despite the expense they wanted to record *Carmen*. DG would negotiate directly with Lenny and all the principals, but I would deliver the orchestra, chorus, and comprimarios at basic union minimums. The Met's share of royalties would be small but I nevertheless felt that this was a heaven-sent opportunity to get the company once again into a studio and before the record-buying public, and with a production that stood an enormous chance of being a huge success.

I agreed to Mowrey's proposal and began threading my way through the fourteen unions representing the Met's professional employees. I came a cropper, however, with the chorus. They wanted double union minimums, which were, of course, out of the question, since it would mean having to pass the same on to everyone else. I looked carefully over the chorus contract and discovered that if they turned down a legitimate offer for a recording based on union scale, the Met was free to hire another group. I met with their representatives, repeated the DG offer, and was turned down a second time.

"I'm sorry, but you leave me no choice," I said to them. "I'll hire an outside chorus."

"You wouldn't dare," they replied.

"Watch me," I said, and I did.

Carmen took ten sessions to record and cost Deutsche Grammophon $275,000, a staggering sum for a classical recording at the time. It sold more than one hundred thousand copies within the first few years and became DG's best-selling opera. It has recently been rereleased on CD and continues its winning and successful ways.

By the time the recording was completed, my life was totally devoted to running the Metropolitan Opera. Immediately after Gentele's death, the board appointed me acting general manager; in 1973 I was given the full title and responsibility. It was a fascinating and time-consuming job and, except for trustee meetings on Lenny's affairs, I saw very little of him. We did meet for the occasional Sunday brunch, when Felicia, Lenny, and I would gossip a little and relax in each other's company, and once in a while the four of us would sneak off to the theater. Harry Kraut, now aided and abetted by Paul Epstein, who had become Lenny's lawyer shortly after Abe Friedman's death, had taken up Amberson's managerial reins with considerable dispatch and intelligence.

It was at one of our Sunday brunches in early 1973 that we met once again to discuss a project, this time involving not Lenny but Felicia.

At their dining table I began to describe an upcoming production of Berlioz's *Les Troyens*, a first for the Metropolitan, which we were planning for the 1973–1974 season. *Les Troyens* is an enormous work requiring huge forces: an orchestra of 120, a chorus of at least 110, 22 principal parts, a large corps de ballet, acrobats, and numerous supers. Andromache, one of the principal roles, is a nonspeaking, nonsinging part requiring special skills. She must command the stage by sheer force of personality in one demanding scene while every eye, both onstage and off, is trained on her. The part calls for a sympathetic portrayal of tragic elegance.

I was looking at Felicia while I was describing the role and suddenly realized all over again that she'd given up her own successful acting career when she married Lenny.

"What about you?" I said. "You've been away from the stage too long. This is the perfect comeback role!"

She laughed, but I could see by her eyes she was interested.

"Look," I said, "don't make up your mind now. I'll call in a day or so for your answer. I'm absolutely serious. I know the director is a fan of yours and will be delighted with the suggestion."

Lenny leaned over and took her hand.

"It's a great idea. Among other things, if you decide to do it, we'll each have one of those Met Opera posters marked with our debuts!"

The next morning I called Nathaniel Merrill, *Les Troyens*'s stage director, and made the suggestion. He liked the idea but before committing himself wanted to meet her. I called Felicia, who by now was quite interested in the role, and made a date with Merrill. They met, liked each other, and the part was hers.

On opening night Lenny joined us in my box. I had to keep telling him to be quiet. Only when Felicia made her entrance did he shut up completely. There she was, one lovely woman, holding a small boy by the hand and surrounded by two hundred people on the stage. All eyes were on her as she moved gracefully through a most touching scene accompanied by spectacularly beautiful music from the orchestra. She was perfection. Then, at her exit, Lenny turned to us and said jubilantly: "There you are! That's it for *this* opera. After Felicia, everything from here on is straight downhill!" He jumped up, kissed all the people seated in the box—and left. I could cheerfully have murdered him.

Happily, *Les Troyens* was a great success. Felicia received wonderful reviews and began thinking seriously about resuming her career. Unfortunately, although her career was beginning to rebloom, her marriage to Lenny was not. In the fall of 1976 the news became public: the Bernsteins had separated.

The news shocked all their friends, coming as it did just weeks after the disastrous opening of Lenny's only collaboration with Alan Jay Lerner, a musical they wrote together for the United States bicentennial called *1600 Pennsylvania Avenue*.

For some years before, however, it had been obvious that Lenny's sexual ambivalence was becoming increasingly difficult for his family. He'd never lied about these feelings, but he had remained circumspect and, for a very public man, had managed to keep that side of his life at a distance. Now firmly in late middle age, and hating growing older, he became caught up in the sexual revolution of the 1970s. As he told a press conference, "there comes a time in life when a man must be what he really is." The marital separation, though, was just that; there were no plans for divorce.

It was a troubling time for both of them and for their children, but by May 1977 they were back together only to be struck by tragedy in July: Felicia became seriously ill with lung cancer.

She was a brave and extraordinary woman and put up a strong fight against the disease. When she felt up to it, I would visit in the late afternoon for a cup of tea. She was always interested in my family and, one Sunday morning, just before Christmas, I brought Betty's and my first grandchild with me as we delivered some of Betty's Christmas cookies, for many years great favorites in the Bernstein household. Felicia and Lenny were having breakfast, and when young Simeon Chapin and I walked in, they both embraced him and me with tears in their eyes.

"The next generation!" she said with great emotion. "How wonderful for you." Her eyes were shining with much beauty, and sadness. "I'll never live to see mine."

Felicia died on 16 June 1978. Lenny, to his dying day, never got over his feelings of guilt and remorse. After her death he plunged back into his work with a driving intensity, in many cases spurred by memories of her.

We began once again to work together on his personal affairs when I left the Metropolitan and became dean of the School of the Arts at Columbia University. Felicia's death made it necessary for him to write a new will. Since aging and dying were always anathema to him, he rebelled at the idea. It took some months before the combined persuasion of Harry, Paul, and myself convinced him he had to do it. With Paul at his side, he finally completed the document, but then he refused to sign it. Nothing Paul or Harry said could budge him. Finally I was asked to try.

I went to see him one afternoon and found him in his study, sitting behind his desk, looking at correspondence. I noticed that the will was parked along the left side of his desk blotter. We chatted about this and that for a while, and finally I asked him:

"Are those blue-bound papers your new will?"

"Yes," he replied suspiciously, "and I'm not going to sign them. I can't bear the thought. I'm just not going to do it."

"Good!" I said. "Forget it. I know how you feel. It's sort of tidying up arrangements for death."

He looked warily at me. "I thought you came here to make me sign," he said.

165

"I did, but I've changed my mind," I replied. I paused, I thought, dramatically.

"You should leave everything just the way it is. Then when you're hit by a bus or run over by a taxi or more probably killed by your own lousy driving, you can take great satisfaction in knowing that most of your hard-earned estate will end up with Uncle Sam."

He stared back at me, chewing on his lower lip. After a minute or two he moved the papers to the center of his desk. I seized my opportunity:

"Paul is downstairs in his apartment [he lived in the same building] with a couple of witnesses and can be up here any moment."

He smiled, appraising my performance.

"OK," he said. "You, with your innocent face. But don't say another word on the subject."

He got up to go to the bathroom. I called Paul and told him the coast was clear. I then shouted my good-byes and left. Afterward I found I'd been named one of his executors.

Afterthoughts

Who, then, was this man Leonard Bernstein?

Since his death I've been puzzling over this question. Although he was physically small—a bundle of power and energy packed into a tiny frame—he was larger than life: for him to have passed anywhere in the world unnoticed would have been, to quote Michael MacLiammoir describing Oscar Wilde, a "most ostentatious form of obscurity." He was a wunderkind until he became an old man. As André Previn observed to Michael Freedland: "Leonard Bernstein skipped middle age. He went from being Lenny to the grand old man in one jump. He was Lenny longer than anyone could be

Lenny. But he made it work. He skipped middle age entirely."

He was, without question, one of the greatest figures in the history of American music. Lenny came as close as any twentieth-century musician to uncovering the universal meaning and the heart of America's diverse musical experiences. He brought these to the entire world; the world embraced him. Music in America will never be the same again.

How do I explain the impact of Leonard Bernstein on me? How do I explain my love for this colorful, explosive, wildly talented, sometimes impossible man?

I lived through many momentous world events with him: after the assassination of his friend John F. Kennedy, when he comforted the nation by conducting the Mahler *Resurrection* Symphony on television, and, a few years later, after Robert Kennedy's death, when he shared the Adagietto from Mahler's Fifth Symphony with the Kennedy family and the rest of the world. When we were in Austria together, I looked on as he publicly saluted the election victory of his friend Bruno Kreisky, the first Jew to become Chancellor of Austria. I was proud of his friendship with Jimmy Carter and the very real help he gave that president on a difficult diplomatic mission to Mexico, where, after a stiff, formal reception following a special concert, he talked the Mexican and American presidents into sitting down together and, with his fluent

Spanish and knowledge of Mexican culture, charmed them into friendship.

I winced for him at Tom Wolfe's phrase "radical chic," coined after a party Felicia gave to raise funds for legal aid to help the Black Panthers; I winced in a different way at a party given in London by Edward Heath, at 10 Downing Street, after a benefit concert, when he hugged the prime minister and asked: "And how is your tottering government tonight?" I blushed at his excessive behavior during a dinner given by New York's Mayor Ed Koch toward the end of the Iranian hostage crisis, when he and the mayor took opposite sides on the ransom payments being offered in the last days of the Carter administration.

I was never what might be called a "playtime pal." Early in our relationship I made it obvious that I didn't like late nights or long drawn-out parties. After concerts abroad I dreaded piling into cars and being driven God knows where for just one more little drink or supper; in this country I ducked as often as I could the myriad guests and fans and sycophants who streamed into his dressing room, elbowing one another for better access to the maestro, who would sit in a short bathrobe, Scotch in one hand, cigarette in the other, receiving obeisance like an Asian pasha. I was never the one called for a quick squash game, an impromptu supper, a round of anagrams, or when he had a sudden craving for a hot dog, but I was often the one called when he needed to talk about family matters or had backed himself into a touchy situation and needed help untangling potential complications.

From the day we met until the day he died, our relationship was based on some arcane chemistry that can best be described as instinctive trust coupled with mutual affection. I envied him his grace and talent and power to hold people spellbound with an art as vital to me as bread and water and breathing; he envied what he viewed as my basic optimism and peace of mind, although I was the one with the ulcers, and he roared through life abusing his body with few visible effects, emerging stronger each year. In truth I think he was fascinated by my family, with American roots going back over 350 years and the sense of continuity this implied. He wanted his own sense of American strengths and security and found a reasonable example of this in our relationship. He once said that when professional matters had been agreed upon by Harry Kraut and myself, he never gave them a second thought. Once, at a Players Club dinner in my honor, Lenny elaborated on this theme to such an extent that Harold Rome, the master of ceremonies, asked him if he really believed what he was saying. He made it clear that he did. Perhaps, too, there was a large part of what his brother Burton summed up succinctly and beautifully in his eulogy: "He wanted the whole world to love itself into one big happy family and took it as a personal affront when the world refused to comply. He maintained unflinching optimism and religious trust in the ultimate improvability of man, despite all the hard evidence to the contrary. Lenny was in love with love."

The Danes have a wonderful expression: "To live in hearts we leave behind is not to die." Leonard Bernstein could never die. He lives in too many hearts.

INDEX

✄ I N D E X ✄

✥ INDEX ✥